LEAD LIKE A HUMAN

LEAD LIKE A HUMAN

PRACTICAL STEPS TO BUILDING HIGHLY ENGAGED TEAMS

ADAM WEBER

Advantage®

Published by Advantage, Charleston, South Carolina.
Member of Advantage Media Group.

ADVANTAGE is a registered trademark, and the Advantage colophon is a trademark of Advantage Media Group, Inc.

Printed in the United States of America.

10 9 8 7 6 5 4 3 2 1

ISBN: 978-1-64225-170-8
LCCN: 2020910010

Cover design by David Taylor.
Layout design by Megan Elger.

This publication is designed to provide accurate and authoritative information in regard to the subject matter covered. It is sold with the understanding that the publisher is not engaged in rendering legal, accounting, or other professional services. If legal advice or other expert assistance is required, the services of a competent professional person should be sought.

Advantage Media Group is proud to be a part of the Tree Neutral® program. Tree Neutral offsets the number of trees consumed in the production and printing of this book by taking proactive steps such as planting trees in direct proportion to the number of trees used to print books. To learn more about Tree Neutral, please visit **www.treeneutral.com**.

Advantage Media Group is a publisher of business, self-improvement, and professional development books and online learning. We help entrepreneurs, business leaders, and professionals share their Stories, Passion, and Knowledge to help others Learn & Grow. Do you have a manuscript or book idea that you would like us to consider for publishing? Please visit **advantagefamily.com** or call **1.866.775.1696**.

To my wife, Cara,
who has seen the true me throughout every step of my journey.

CONTENTS

ACKNOWLEDGMENTS

To my "original team": Ian, Chris, Kayla, Matt, and Logan. Thank you for taking a chance on a first-time leader. Your belief in me changed my career. The reason I am able to write this book is because of you.

To my mom and dad. Thank you for instilling in me a deep sense of direction and purpose.

To my sons Truett and Callum. You help me find my inner child and make my life full of joy and laughter.

To my business partner Santiago. We've made each other better. Thank you for believing in me and pushing me to become the very best version of myself.

To Nicole MacLean. You saw the vision for this book and helped make it a reality. This wouldn't have happened without you. Thank you!

To my mentors: Chip Neidigh, Christine Kaszubski, Brian Kavicky, Jade Sherer, Jim Marsden, and Todd Richardson. Thank you for caring enough to help me grow.

FOREWORD

by Verne Harnish

When I was a teenager, I worked with the famous archeologist Cynthia Irwin-Williams at the Salmon ruins in New Mexico. Nine hundred years after the construction of the Chacoan pueblo, the team excavated over one-third of the pueblo, recovering almost 1.5 million artifacts from the site. Williams's trained eye took seemingly basic pieces of pottery, instruments, and tools and turned them into stories, revealing the intricacies of this civilization. Reflecting back, it was amid the dirt and dust in the pueblo that I learned the importance of a well-executed discovery process.

Too often, leaders oversimplify. From purpose statements to core values, even our own development, we sacrifice depth for generalizations and simplicities. But when you oversimplify you lose the richness, the edges of what makes a culture truly unique and reveals the bigger story. Understanding and then activating what's in the edges is critical to unlocking opportunities for your organization.

I like to remind people that that word, *organization*, shares its root with the word organism. What leaders have to realize is that this entity is its own kind of living being with its own unique fingerprint and its own personality, comprised of the unique attributes of the individuals who work for you. That's why it's so important to do a discovery exercise so that you truly understand and respect the uniqueness of the organism you're leading.

The discovery process of an archeologist is not unlike the practices originally outlined by the great Jim Collins. Just as Cynthia Irwin-Williams and her team identified artifacts to ascertain what was going on hundreds of years ago, leaders must also leverage their own artifacts, in this case their employees, to discern the true nature of their culture.

As you embark on your own discovery, be open to what you could learn. The essence of archeology is that when you're looking for one thing, you find another. When you're doing an archeological dig, you often find duplicates and hundreds of items that don't really matter, but then you'll get something that's really interesting—something that illuminates a part of the culture you never knew or couldn't exactly name—and that's the fun part of this discovery process.

It's apparent that, throughout his journey, Adam has done the work of a genuine discovery process, both in his personal development and in the organizations he's led. His vulnerability about his own successes and failures gives you an example of what it means to lead like a human. With each experience he's learned necessary lessons to succeed in the role he's in today and to appreciate the needs of others. After all, you can't lead like a human until you understand humans.

I love that *Human* is in the title of this book. Leaders are constantly searching for that secret to success or plug-'n'-play playbook, but the truth is that there is no silver bullet. If you're hoping to find that here, then this isn't the book for you. Adam has learned, as I have, that discovering and leveraging the nuances of your team unlocks results. Of course, he'll share resources and tips, but there's this wonderful undercurrent about the work needed to be done to better understand yourself and your team; embrace this discovery process. As you read this book, recognize these layers and that the true learning will be in the nuanced application for your unique organization.

UNLOCK YOUR POTENTIAL

I t's probably fair to say that I've had more jobs than Forrest Gump. I've been a salesperson, an academic advisor, a pastor, and even a traveling musician. If you saw my LinkedIn page, you might think, "What in the world is this guy doing?" Indeed, I've worn so many proverbial hats in my day that it's hard for me to even track what I've done in what year. But these roles have all brought their own challenges and achievements that have led me to where I am today.

Hi! My name is Adam Weber, and I cofounded Emplify, an employee-engagement measurement company created to help people achieve their true potential at work. While my career path has been decidedly wandering, today I am intentional about where my life journey is leading me. It might have taken me many years, but I finally have the answer to the question, "What do I want to do every day?" The answer: I want to help people achieve their true potential and become the very best version of themselves.

Today, people don't often know what they could become. All too often, today's employees find themselves in unfulfilling jobs where they waste away the hours between 9:00 a.m. and 5:00 p.m. These dead-end jobs are draining the life out of our people. They do meaningless tasks to check a box without understanding how they're moving the business forward or what impact their work is having. Their idleness, however, is not always their fault—it is due to lack of true leadership in their organizations. Their managers are not mentors helping them achieve greatness but stumbling blocks impeding an employee's journey at every turn.

This has led to a culture where managers spur their teams along with brute force, frustration, and dated leadership tactics. They dictate their demands from behind closed boardroom doors and expect the employees under them to execute on their orders immediately. They believe that they have the answers to every business question and that they alone have those answers. They think it a waste of time or unwise to ask their team for input and would never share their own shortcomings with their staff. I don't mean to scare you, but these managers are everywhere, in every industry, and they are wreaking havoc on your organizations right now. They stifle the productivity and growth of individuals and limit the bottom line of your businesses. But how do we solve this problem? How can we transform these monster managers into something more beneficial for you and your employees?

In both my successes and failures, I've discovered how to lead people in ways that grow both the business and the employee. My hope is that by transparently sharing my journey, I can nudge you along on yours, helping you become more of the leader you were meant to be and in turn creating teams of people who bring their best selves to work every day. And when you fill your teams with motivated people, great things will start happening for your company. This might sound like an uphill climb, but trust me: it's simpler than it seems. **It all starts with leading like a human**.

While I've honed my own leadership practices over my professional career, my mission to maximize the potential in people is a highly personal one. It was inspired by someone incredibly close to me: my mom. In a way, to know me is to know my mom. Her courage, humility, and leadership cultivated in me a deep conviction to help and guide those whom I come across. The lessons she taught me through her actions affected me in ways I am still realizing to this day.

Surrounded by poverty and addiction, my mom grew up next to the coal mines in rural Maybeury, West Virginia, population under one thousand. Unlike the fictional Mayberry, her hometown was the opposite of idyllic Americana. When I was a boy, she took me to the house she'd grown up in. I remember washing machines lined up across the creek that ran in front of her house, serving as a makeshift bridge from her home to the country road running through town. That road went to one of the only buildings in town: the post office. On that trip, I saw how the residents of Maybeury made what they could from what little they had. Each and every one of them struggled to get by and get unstuck from the depression of Maybeury.

In the Maybeury of my mother's childhood, if you had a job, it was somehow related to coal mining. Coal was the backbone of the US economy at that time and provided jobs to countless workers across Appalachia. As she grew into a teenager, however, society was beginning to shift away from coal. As this once-booming industry began to decline across the United States, for Maybeury, this meant a sudden scarcity of jobs and a suffering economy. Many of the town residents found themselves without a job and, what was worse, no education to help them find another career. My mom realized from a young age that

> My mom realized from a young age that education gives you more than just knowledge—it gives you the freedom to choose what your life can be.

education gives you more than just knowledge—it gives you the freedom to choose what your life can be.

Instead of resigning herself to her own circumstances, she leaned into the hand she'd been dealt. She knew that in order to get out, she'd have to put in twice the effort; she challenged herself because no one else was going to. In high school, she studied hard and excelled as a star student. She became the first person from my family to graduate college, where she got a degree in teaching from Ball State University in Muncie, Indiana. After she graduated, she taught in the poorest neighborhoods of Muncie and was committed to helping children raised in poverty find their own way out.

Growing up, I remember how she'd take in her students, going so far as to invite them into our homes when they had nowhere else to go. One of her students, in fact, became my foster brother and lived with us for several years. I watched her as she coached and mentored these kids into becoming the best versions of themselves. She knew what it was like to grow up with nothing, and she wanted to show every kid she taught that they had a chance, and she would be there to guide them on their new path.

I still carry the lessons my mother imparted in me. At the core, she taught me two things: your current circumstance is not your permanent circumstance, and when you find the way you can affect others, lean into it and spend your life doing that work. Her principles and strength have been my true north, guiding me to where I am now. To me, my mom embodied what it meant to lead like a human. I've read countless books on leadership and have experienced a wide spectrum of bosses, but none of them have been as influential as my mother's approach to caring and nurturing the people around her. She showed me that when you help people see their own potential, you unlock in them a passion for growth that is unstoppable. And that is what it means to lead like a human. It's a radically different approach to leadership than what you'll find in other books on leadership. As you go through the chapters ahead, I hope this book will give you permission to shed what you think a leader should be and lead like a human.

When you help people see their own potential, you unlock in them a passion for growth that is unstoppable.

During my career, I've met folks who've encouraged and lifted me up. I've also encountered people who have—shall I say—done the exact opposite. In each of these interactions, I've gathered examples of both excellent and poor management. These anecdotes, combined with years of trial-and-error leadership, have helped me create what I believe is a simple yet effective plan for leading teams in the modern workforce. *Lead Like a Human* is a practical guide to building highly engaged teams by being a genuine and authentic leader focused on drawing out the very best in those you manage. This book will help you create the teams you've dreamed of while leading in a way that will bring out the best in you too.

CHAPTER ONE

THE ACCIDENTAL ENTREPRENEUR

If there is an aroma
faint in the evening breeze
take a grateful breath and
move in that direction.
Your road will be there,
glowing in the moonlight.
Your compass rose has opened.
You must go north.

—"True North," by Doug von Koss (abridged)

The first step of my journey toward leading like a human started in a church. Well, when I say "step," it was more of a stumble. The church was called Commonway and was located in Muncie, outside Indianapolis. At first I was just the music leader in the church, but a series of events beyond my control led to me becoming the pastor of this congregation. It was in this little church in Muncie where I'd find out who I was truly supposed to be. My time at Commonway taught me valuable lessons that shaped me into the entrepreneur and leader I am today.

People often ask me how I went from being a pastor of a small community church to an entrepreneur who cofounded a people-engagement company. I admit it doesn't seem like an obvious career shift. The candid answer is that both of these roles came to be by accident, but not a "whoops" one like stepping on a LEGO or knocking over a glass of water in a restaurant. These accidents were more like opportunistic moments that spurred me to grow, even if I didn't recognize that at the time. I had the willingness to say yes in these tough situations, which helped me become a fast learner despite the chaotic and uncertain times. In the midst of these moments, I found my true purpose and felt something unlock in me—a desire to lead.

When I first joined Commonway, I never intended nor dreamed that I'd one day be the pastor there. At the time, I was making my living as a wandering musician, and I came to the church one Sunday on a whim. My girlfriend, Cara, and I had recently moved to the neighborhood and were looking for ways to become involved in the community. Almost immediately, we were greeted by the young pastor who led the small church. He wasn't that much older than me, but already he had a community who looked to him for guidance. He was searching for someone to play the guitar and lead worship songs during services. As a wayward musician, I was shocked when he asked if I'd take on the gig. He offered me a hundred dollars a week, which, at the time, was an incredibly generous offer. I hadn't expected to walk into Commonway and find work as a musician, but there it was—an opportunity waiting for me to take it.

Back then, the congregation was tiny—only about twelve folks and the young pastor. Commonway, however, had a leader with a strong vision. This young man, who wasn't even thirty yet, wanted to create a church that would be welcoming and unique. I admired his conviction and the passion he brought to this endeavor. It wasn't long before I knew I wanted to help him realize his dream of creating a new kind of church community. Everyone at Commonway did. It was an exciting time, and the entire congregation was all in. It felt amazing to be making something of value surrounded by passionate folks.

As Cara and I became more involved in the church, we began to know these folks intimately. Most of them were young people on their own journeys who'd come to Commonway to fill their own individual needs. Whether that was community or something deeper, the church and its pastor sought to make a home where its people could be their best selves. I saw in the pastor a real desire to help these people and was reminded of how my mother had worked with her students. Before too long, I was asked to help out as the music minister at Commonway—a staff position and a step up from my role as the musician. That being said, the Commonway "staff" consisted of only two people: myself and the pastor. Nevertheless, we were determined to create a space of growth for these people whom we'd come to call family.

Over the next year, our congregation grew from twelve to over 250. Our little church was full of folks crammed into our small auditorium on mismatched chairs and couches pulled from different rooms. People from all walks of life came to Commonway just to see what it was all about. Even the mayor and his family were there during Sunday services. My position as the music leader was becoming a real job—although I believe the pay stayed around a hundred dollars a week. Doing good, it must be said, doesn't always pay the bills.

During this time, the pastor and I would often exchange amazed looks at the number of people coming through our doors. Commonway had struck something in the community, and the people were turning up in droves. The church that I helped grow had become a home not only to me and my family, but to many others as well. Real adults with real kids were coming to Sunday services. Commonway was feeling more and more like a legitimate church, despite the fact that the pastor and I were making it up as we went along ("Fake it till you make it").

Three years went by. Cara and I got engaged. And I continued to lead the music each Sunday morning while we prepared for our wedding day. One Saturday in 2007, a week before the ceremony, I received a call. It was my young pastor friend. He confessed to me that he had made a terrible mistake, and felt it was wise to officially step down from his position. As the only staff member, I was told *I'd* be taking over as the pastor of Commonway Church. I was suddenly promoted from music minister to pastor, and I had less than twenty-four hours to write a sermon for the next morning. This would be the first sermon I'd ever have to write, and I had to do so with no formal training. Let me tell you—I was in way over my head.

Something you need to know about me is that, at this time, I had kind of wandered through life, from opportunity to opportunity. I didn't have a clear plan of what I wanted to do—unlike Cara, who has diligently been working on her dream of being an architect since she was a little girl. It's a quality of hers that I've always loved, because I know I've never had it. But now, I was being called upon by my community to step up to a position that I had no experience in. I was stunned at what to do. I mean, think about it: I had gone from a guy on the street with a guitar to the pastor of a church where the mayor went for spiritual guidance.

From the moment I heard that my friend was stepping down, I could see this home and all we had spent three years building together beginning to crumble apart. I thought about canceling the service the next morning, but I knew I couldn't. It would mean the end of Commonway—not just for me but for the entire congregation. I thought about calling it quits and stepping down myself, but then I thought about these people and how much they needed that home. Determined, I put aside what I was doing and wrote that first sermon.

The next morning, I walked into the church so nervous that I was shaking. I tried to calm myself before I entered the auditorium, but it didn't help. I couldn't shake my own feeling of inadequacy. Our sermons at Commonway were conducted in the round, which meant that I stood in the middle of the group and spoke to a crowd who completely surrounded me. I stood in the middle of these 250 congregants and could feel their eyes on me. Not everyone had heard the news, so I had to be the first to break it to them. The pastor had stepped down, and I was taking over. My voice almost cracked; my mouth was bone dry.

I felt so woefully underprepared. Who was I to speak and have all these folks hang on to my every word? That being said, I knew I couldn't just sit there in silence. I unfolded the small paper in my hand and looked down at the sermon I had written the night before. When I looked up, something had changed in the way I saw these people. I could feel that I was holding these folks—their hopes and fears, aspirations and doubts. I felt the weight and the sadness of an entire group of people on my shoulders. But instead of giving up, I breathed deep and leaned into the discomfort.

After I finished the sermon, I walked off the stage and into a back room where there was a small closet in the corner. Without thinking, I opened the door to the closet and then shut it behind me, cloaking myself in darkness. As the door closed, I felt a well of emotion open up inside me and pour out in a big blubbery mess. I was crying, and it was because I was exhausted. What I couldn't see then, however, was that I wasn't just exhausted—I was changing. On that Sunday, I was becoming the person I was meant to be, and that outpouring of emotion was a result of feeling the pain that comes with growth. I was discovering my personal mission.

When I think back on that Sunday, it's clear to me that I was being stretched. I had been pushed to the edge of my ability for the first time, and I realized what I was truly capable of. That day was the pivotal moment when I stopped wandering and started doing what I was made to do. And I didn't find that moment in myself. I found it in the faces and hearts of my congregants, who leaned on me for guidance. I realized that by doing the hard and scary thing with humility, I had become the leader my community needed.

Before that day, I don't think I'd ever worked hard. To speak candidly, life was a thing that just kind of happened to me. I breezed through school by leaning on intellect rather than effort. In college, I went to class when I was supposed to but also never missed a chance to jam with my bandmates. While at the end of my four years my degree said sociology, I really had a triple major in playing music, making friends, and playing video games. My area of expertise was in original Nintendo, and, if you must ask, I play a mean Tecmo Bowl.

My life wasn't hard, but it was aimless. Thanks to my parents, I had a good upbringing. They shielded me from the poverty and difficulties that my mother endured. The trials she had been through gave her a strong passion to help others. I had witnessed this trait in her but hadn't fully comprehended it until that day. When I spoke to those 250 people in that church, I felt what my mother had instilled in me as a child coming to life—a passion for unlocking the true potential in people. I found that as a pastor, but today, as a leader and entrepreneur, I still try to live my life by those values she inspired in me.

If my time at Commonway stretched me by throwing me into a situation unprepared, my time as an entrepreneur taught me the importance of trying, learning, and trying again when you are starting something new. Opportunities come at you quickly, and you need to be ready to take them on. And that is an incredibly accurate description of how I met Santiago Jaramillo, now my business partner. It all started with a blog post I'd written years after I left Commonway to pursue a position in sales. He'd stumbled upon my post while he was in his last semester of college. Santi, as he was known to those close to him, reached out to me on Twitter because he was interested in learning more about what I had written and how I understood sales. Little did I know how this chance encounter would alter the course of my life.

"I'm trying to start a business and need to learn sales. I'd love to hear your story. Would you be up for coffee?" I figured that I had nothing to lose, and I was always willing to help out a young person just getting their start. I agreed to meet with him.

The next week, I walked into a nearby Starbucks and saw a bright-eyed young man who was definitely not the typical recent college graduate. The first thing I noticed about Santiago was his incredible charisma. He was charming and affable, but also incredibly serious about the work he was doing. After we both sat down with our coffees, he sketched out a business plan in front of me on a brown Starbucks napkin. While he spoke, I began to realize how truly special and strong this person was.

One of the first things that stood out to me about Santi was his commitment to making the world a better place. As we got to know each other, we discovered that we shared a passion for creating businesses that could make a global impact. Santi was brilliant and energetic and had a drive that I'd lacked at his age. He worked hard because he knew he had meaningful work to do. He had ideas but also the plan to get them done. His own excitement spread to everyone with whom he worked. For a moment, I was reminded of the passion of the folks at Commonway setting out to start something new. After that first coffee in mid-July 2011, I called my wife and told her, "I think I'll be working for that kid someday."

The next day, I went back to my sales job. I was working on a couple of pitches to new customers, but my mind kept wandering back to Santiago and his project. It was a solid idea. He knew how the business would run and had a vision for how it could disrupt the industry. The problem was that he only had one customer. And a business with just one customer is … well … mostly an idea. Throughout my day, I kept jotting down new ideas to help him get customers quickly—almost like doodles in the margin of a school notebook. That night, I called up Santi and told him it was time for our next coffee. I couldn't wait to share these ideas, because I hoped it would help him along.

We met for coffee again, and, almost immediately, the pens hit the napkins. This time, it was me drawing out a sales strategy for him. I had thought through his offerings and the problems they solved. I showed him some outlines for how I thought he could grow and scale. I realized I was getting excited by his prospects and what starting this business would mean for him. Halfway through our meeting, he stopped me, looked me straight in the eyes, and said, "You have to do this with me."

I had never thought about starting a company before. It had always been my life's work to support others—my time at Commonway showed me that. Now, however, with this recent graduate sitting in front of me, I had the opportunity to start something new—something fresh and something that could be mine. Once again, I was hearing a call similar to the one that I'd heard at Commonway. Those coffee chats and scribbles on napkins were beginning to take the form of something much larger than Santi or myself. I had accidentally become an entrepreneur with this recently graduated whiz kid.

But building a new business wouldn't be easy. I knew it would take a lot of my time, with a tremendous risk of failure. I had a family to support and a mortgage to pay too. Putting the pen down, I told Santiago, "I'd love to, but you'll have to sell my wife on it."

The next day, he showed up to my house with a slide-deck presentation and a very elaborate spreadsheet. My wife opened the meeting. "So, you graduated college last month and you want to offer my husband a job?" Our sons—three and four years old—were playing with their fire trucks beside us. A stray block thrown from the youngest landed right in front of Santi before he had the chance to answer. Shaken, he paused for a moment and then started his presentation.

Sitting in our living room, he went through his proposal and explained exactly why he needed a business partner and how I could help. He was talking faster than an auctioneer. Before long, I could tell he was sweating. While on the surface he looked calm and composed, I later found out he was so nervous that he'd soaked through his undershirt.

Cara is not like me, and that's why I love her. While I am impulsive, she's methodical. While I think with my heart and let its impulses guide me, Cara is a practical woman with a brilliant mind for planning. Throughout the meeting, my wife took in everything Santi was saying—listening intently, nodding when appropriate, and taking notes when needed. At the end of the speedy presentation, he opened up the floor for questions. She looked down at her notepad, took a breath, and said, "I do have one question. Will we have insurance?"

Santi paused, coughed, and blurted out, "Of course, of course. He'll have insurance." (Cut to Santi, fifteen minutes later, fanning his soaked undershirt and googling "How do you set up insurance for employees?" in his car parked in our driveway.) The presentation completed, we ushered our guest to the front door to say good night and that we'd be in touch. After the door closed, Cara turned to me and said, "Adam, if you don't do this, you'll regret it for the rest of your life."

Two weeks later, I joined as a cofounder of Bluebridge, our napkin idea turned company. We built a mobile engagement platform for nonprofit organizations. Within our first year, we had over a hundred customers, but for two people with big dreams, we'd chosen too small of a market. While sales were growing rapidly, what I really found myself drawn to was my position as leader of a team. Of course, I loved growing the business, but I loved growing my team even more.

At first, I started with a team of five folks who were about the same age as Santiago. For most of them, it was their first job right out of college. For me, it was my first time being a manager. By now you probably see the trend here: first an accidental pastor, then an accidental entrepreneur; and now, at Bluebridge, I was an accidental manager. With my team, however, I never wanted them to feel like accidents I had to handle. I wanted to lead them with intention and purpose.

I decided that what I needed to do was to completely invest myself in these people. Their journey was my journey. When they stumbled, I stumbled too. We were learning together, and I became committed to seeing them grow. I knew that the only way for our business to accomplish its goals would be to train and motivate my team to create something exceptional.

Our business was moving fast. More and more customers joined us, and, in turn, more employees came to us as well. I began to feel that same excitement that I'd had at Commonway as the church filled with new congregants. As the company grew, we took on new capabilities—ultimately shifting our mission away from mobile app development. We became more interested in how we engaged the people using our product and how good people do good work. Inspired by this new mission, some of our team members started experimenting with our platform and ended up building a mobile app to improve internal communication. At first, it was only for our use, but before long both Santi and I realized how powerful this tool could be.

That was the start of Emplify—an organization dedicated to employee engagement. From the beginning, Santi and I knew that our people were what made our company special. We did everything we could to encourage our staff and give them the opportunity to work on projects that excited them. When they came to us with their idea for Emplify, we realized right away they were onto something. People engagement was a topic that combined our passion to make the world a better place with solid business acumen. In addition, it opened up a market for us that was large enough to fulfill our goals of growing a big business.

So we made a bold decision. We sold Bluebridge for $8 million and invested every single penny of it into Emplify. I knew we had to be all in, or else it wouldn't succeed. When I first started at Bluebridge, I was enamored by the thought of a big exit someday and reaping a big reward from selling my start-up. My time with my team, however, made me realize that the thrill of making a profit off my start-up investment was just that—a thrill. Selling Bluebridge could have just been another stop on my wandering path, but I could feel something awakening in me that was the culmination of my years spent drifting from moment to moment, job to job. A style of leadership that challenged me to create meaningful moments of growth for people at any stage of their career.

As I mentioned before, my mom always taught me that helping people was the greatest thing someone could do. In everything I'd done up until this time, I'd found myself feeling most "myself" when I was doing just that. As a pastor at Commonway, I'd found my passion for leading and inspiring others. As a manager at Bluebridge, my team showed me that I truly loved investing in and developing people. Both of these experiences unlocked in me my true purpose—helping people achieve their true potential. That was the heart of what Emplify came to stand for and spurred in us a question that has inspired the book you're now holding in your hands: How do you lead people to do good work that will challenge their heads and captivate their hearts?

> People are the very foundation of your business, but if they aren't bringing the whole of themselves to their work, if they aren't engaged, then how can you expect them to drive meaningful performance for your business?

While we work on this problem every day at Emplify, it has ramifications for organizations of all kinds. People are the very foundation of your business, but if they aren't bringing the whole of themselves to their work, if they aren't engaged, then how can you expect them to drive meaningful performance for your business? This question of engagement is one that business leaders are always trying to solve. They desperately try quick-fix solutions to deep-rooted issues that are preventing them from achieving their business goals. And yes,

I'm looking at your Nerf guns, Ping-Pong tables, and liquor at the company holiday party.

Today, it's been about four years since Santiago and I first took this big step in Emplify. We spend every day trying to get to the bottom of these engagement problems for organizations from almost every industry, and I love every single minute of it. It took me a long time, and a bit of wandering, but I'm finally doing the work I was meant to do. That is the most important thing. It's always been about developing people for me, and I get to come into work every day and do just that.

Throughout my life, I've walked a winding path in my own personal journey of fulfillment. I've led groups with diverse goals, passions, and perspectives. I've been led by an assortment of managers—the good, the bad, and the unbearable. I've even coached leaders on how to best guide and develop their people to move their organizations forward. While my career choices have evolved, one thing in my life has remained constant: my passion and understanding of good leadership. And it starts by leading your people as a human.

From my time as a pastor to my time as a people leader, I've come to realize that people are just people. They have their own elemental needs, and they're on their own journeys to fulfill them. But in order to do so, they sometimes need a guide. Someone who's on the same path who can humbly show them the way. They need a leader who is committed and open to unlocking their true potential. A leader who has vision and conviction to encourage them during stretching moments of radical growth. And I'm not talking about just while they're at work. They need someone who sees them as a human and not just a cog in a larger organizational machine.

Throughout this book, you'll find lessons and tips on how to lead like a human. I've compiled these things not just from my own experience but from the data of hundreds of thousands of employees who utilize Emplify. From my early days at Commonway to my current position at Emplify, I have amassed a multitude of stories about leaders and how they've inspired those around them. After you're done reading this book, I hope you'll have absorbed those stories and adapted them into your own practice of leadership.

There's been a shift in the way business operates today compared to years past. A new generation of talent, and increasingly innovative technology, have both created a modern workplace culture that requires new forms of leadership. Those who fail to understand these shifts risk losing employees, customers, and, at worst, their whole business. In a rapidly changing world, leaders who adapt to the needs and desires of their people are the ones who will reap the rewards of a workforce operating at maximum potential. While accidents can often lead to radical growth, underestimating your people is a mishap you can't afford to make.

CHAPTER TWO

A CHANGING WORKFORCE

We don't want tradition. We want to live in the present and the only history that is worth a damn is the history we make today.

—Henry Ford

Early on at Emplify, one of the ways we would spread the word about our approach to people engagement was by sharing our perspective at conferences. For one of these events, I'd been working on a talk about building and keeping engaged talent—a topic I'll get into later in this book. We rolled up to the hotel with our team of twentysomethings and quickly realized we were drawing a lot of attention. The ballroom where I was set to speak was packed with seasoned CEOs craning their necks to get a look at this new company with the young team. Looking around, we all began to think, *Hm. One of these things is not like the other.* It was clear that we were the youngest people in the room by far, and not everyone was exactly comfortable with that. As everyone took their seats, the awkwardness slightly dissipated, and I approached the stage to start my talk.

This was one of the first times I had given this talk, and I was still just getting used to it. You won't be surprised to hear that a lot of what's in this book was in that talk—leading with purpose, unlocking potential, being radically transparent, et cetera, et cetera. The speech was going pretty well, and I felt confident that the audience of leaders was with me. About nine minutes into the talk, I turned the floor over to them and asked what specific people-strategy problems they were facing at their companies. Enter a gentleman in a brown suit who stood up in the crowd and asked me about everyone's favorite topic: millennials.

"What should I do about my millennial staff?" he asked.

I was about to respond when he cut me off with what can only be described as a thirteen-minute diatribe on how millennials were destroying his company. All while the onsite Emplify team, which consisted of millennials, sat and listened to him berate their entire generation.

This man—let's call him Frustrated Frank—wouldn't let it go. He called his younger staff lazy, entitled, and flaky. He cited what he thought was their complete inability to stay at a company for more than two years. He didn't think he owed these people anything if they were just going to quit someday for another opportunity. What's more, he continued, was that he was paying these staff more than enough for them to just—and I quote—"do their damn jobs." At one point, Frank, out of breath, had completely abandoned his original question in an effort to console himself. Looking at those around him, he tried to tell them that if he and people like him just stuck around long enough, they'd win.

"We have to win," he kept saying to himself. Looking back now, I can see how frustrated he was with his situation. He only wanted to fix a problem he felt was looming over him, and his diatribe and finger-pointing were just him grasping for a solution. What Frustrated Frank didn't realize was that the only thing that needed to change was his antiquated thinking, informed by business practices from over two decades ago.

The world has changed a lot over the last twenty years. Think back to the early 2000s. *The Sixth Sense* had just come out, and people were sporting puka shell necklaces and long bleached-blond hair. (I should know: I have pictures of myself to prove it.) Cell phones were large Nokia blocks with no real screen to shatter. T9 texting meant that a "*hi how r u*" message might take minutes to type. And if you were anything like me, you had a friend whom you absolutely had to call at 9:01 p.m. to cash in on your free evening minutes.

Back then, most millennials were at the mall, not in the office. It was their parents who went to nine-to-five jobs in order to bring home the proverbial bacon. They clocked in, did their work, and clocked out every day in an effort to support their families and advance their careers. For these folks, switching jobs wasn't something they did lightly. The idea of employees who spent their entire lives with one company wasn't strange in the slightest. In fact, it was the norm. Office culture became synonymous with boredom and even became the butt of many jokes in pop culture. ("Mondays, am I right?" *Office Space*, 1999.)

Today, office life is certainly … different. While part of this shift can be attributed to new technology (like the internet, for instance), another factor has completely changed the way we're operating our businesses. It's a surge of millennial workers who are quickly surpassing their parents as the largest population in the workforce. By the end of 2020, for example, millennials are projected to represent more than 50 percent of the makeup of a given organization. By 2025, that number will jump to 75 percent.[1] Millennials have become a formidable force in today's workplaces who bring their own ideas and perspectives about work and how it should fit into an employee's life.

> Millennials have become a formidable force in today's workplaces who bring their own ideas and perspectives about work and how it should fit into an employee's life.

Millennials' attitudes about work are completely different from those of their predecessors. Twenty years ago, employees said the most important aspects of work were related to compensation and benefits—things that would make for a stable career. In today's job market, however, that's no longer the case. According to a recent Glassdoor survey, employees cited purpose as one of the most important factors in considering where they worked.[2] In fact, some millennial employees said they would be willing to take a pay cut if they would be doing work that mattered at an organization where they felt their voices would be heard.[3] These workers are looking to their employers for meaningful work that inspires and challenges them, but more often than not, they're being given boring tasks that drive them away.

What might have been satisfactory for an employee twenty years ago is no longer accepted by today's standard, and this imbalance is cultivating an unfortunate apathy in our workforce. It's the main

---

1   Peter Economy, "The Millennial Workplace of the Future Is Almost Here," *Inc.*, January 15, 2019, https://www.inc.com/peter-economy/the-millennial-workplace-of-future-is-almost-here-these-3-things-are-about-to-change-big-time.html.

2   Amanda Stansell, "Which Workplace Factors Drive Employee Satisfaction Around the World?" Glassdoor, July 11, 2019, https://www.glassdoor.com/research/employee-satisfaction-drivers/.

3   Maggie Overfelt, "The New Generation of Employees Would Take Less Pay for These Job Perks," CNBC, May 31, 2017.

cause of the job-hopping that is now a topic of contention in board-rooms across the country. In the worst case, they'll leave a job for one they feel will better suit their needs, and in even worse cases, they'll stay. This apathy causes workers to underperform and underdeliver.

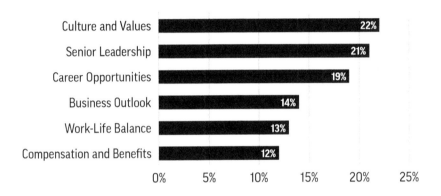

The Workplace Factors That Matter Most to Employee Satisfaction in the U.S.

SOURCE: GLASSDOOR ECONOMIC RESEARCH (GLASSDOOR.COM/RESEARCH)

This isn't just "a millennial thing," like our Frustrated Frank was complaining about. We've also seen older-generation workers beginning to leave if they feel their needs aren't being met. Millennials were simply the catalyst in this workplace revolution. The power dynamic in the job market has shifted, and now employees have much more control than they've ever had. This has lessened the stigma that used to come with leaving a job. And with the advent of the internet, it's never been easier to find a better one.

Smartphone technology has completely transformed the way we connect and the way we pursue new opportunities. Gone is the brick Nokia from twenty years ago; now, the iPhone and other smartphones rule how we communicate with and operate in the world.

These smartphones are ubiquitous in the workplace today because, well, they're practically attached to us, twenty-four seven. Think about where your phone is right now, and I bet it's within reach. Today, employees have that limitless resource for job hunting right at their fingertips, while twenty years ago, finding a job meant printing out a lot of résumés and stuffing plenty of envelopes.

Thanks to mobile job-searching platforms, employees can rate and review their companies and their jobs right from the desks they work at every day. In less than a decade, companies like LinkedIn, Indeed, and Glassdoor have changed the way we seek and talk about jobs. Not only do these platforms allow employees to speak their minds, but they can also research new opportunities without any worry of repercussions or retaliation. Even LinkedIn's "Easy Apply" feature means that employees can apply for a new job with a single click. This constant job-hopping isn't just a nuisance that a business must endure, but a crisis for managers who can't keep their open positions filled.

Nowadays, every organization has a new and purportedly innovative strategy on how to hire and retain talent, with a bent at capturing millennials. Everyone seems obsessed with cracking the code on how to engage this talent pool that grows larger every day. Unfortunately, many of these strategies are full of empty perks and shallow organizational changes, leaving these companies feeling as out of touch as a puka shell necklace. In an effort to implement their strategies, these business leaders emulate Silicon Valley start-ups, filling their offices with snack jars and foosball tables. But without a meaning behind these perks, these strategies do little to keep people around. As someone who leads a company with snack jars in their office, let me tell you that I'd be a complete failure as a leader if that's why people stayed on at Emplify. These perks will feel bankrupt to your employees if you underdeliver on what your employees truly want—work with meaning.

This systemic problem is due to a workplace culture established over sixty years ago. This culture was created based on two things: a rigid power structure and inadequate data. In the past, many businesses were run based on a rigid, almost militaristic hierarchy where what the boss says goes. Managers were seen as generals commanding troops of their staff and leading them into the battle of the marketplace. When it came time to see how the troops were doing, however, these managers struggled to understand the wants and needs of their people. Instead, they settled for a metric based on how satisfied an employee was based on an overly simplistic survey. If employees were satisfied, then nothing changed, and the top-down power structure continued to run the business. But with today's staffing problems, like underperformance and low retention, these managers are realizing that satisfaction isn't cutting it. The Frustrated Franks of the world are just becoming more frustrated, causing them to tighten their grip on their staff. In this vicious circle, it's becoming clear even to them that something needs to change.

As a leader, your people are looking to you to create the culture that will give them the meaningful work that they need. Your employees want to know that what they're doing has value to the community and an impact on the world around them. Khalid Halim, cofounder of Reboot, a coaching company, perhaps says it best: "There is a fundamental shift happening in the way people view work. It's not just a job or a paycheck anymore. Our work is the expression of our natural gifts intersecting with the needs of the world."[4] Your people want to know that what they do matters, and when you give them that purpose, you unlock their potential and

---

4   Khalid Halim, Home page, www.reboot.io/team/khalid-halim/.

create a team of engaged high performers who'll be loyal to your organization and its mission.

The cultural shifts in how we work that have been brought on by millennials and mobile technology have made creating these high-performing teams more than just a simple matter that can be addressed with outdated management methods. I like to claim that I'm the oldest millennial. I was born in January of 1981, which puts me right on a generational cusp. I've lived through these changes myself and have seen how they have affected today's workforce—both through my own career and in my clients' experiences with Emplify. I've worked with managers like Frustrated Frank who struggle to motivate their staff to do good work. I've watched as my colleagues—and even myself—have jumped ship from companies that were taking us for granted. On top of all that, I've even reverted to the old management rulebook of days past when I felt unsure of how to manage my staff.

What I've discovered in my experience of this unique era for our workforce is that there is a deep need for a new kind of leadership. It's not a rigid set of rules where everyone is assigned a duty to fulfill and receive a paycheck for services rendered. It's a compassionate and authentic approach to leadership that will ease the pain of even the most volatile of Franks and create energized teams ready to take on an organization's toughest problems. All these managers need is the permission to lead like a human. In my experience, I've seen that when you show your people that what they do matters, they'll go above and beyond the goals that have been set for them. And it doesn't stop there. Once you show them what they can do, they'll see that the only thing holding them back is themselves.

CHAPTER THREE

LEAD LIKE A HUMAN

Leadership today is about unlearning management
and relearning being human.

—Javier Pladevall, CEO of Volkswagen Audi Retail Spain

I n 2017, business professors Henry Mintzberg and Joseph Lampel had a question: Can you teach leadership, or is it something you need to learn on the job? In order to get to the bottom of their question, they chose nineteen top-performing Harvard Business School alumni who had been published as the superstars of business in 1990. The professors wanted to see if, decades later, the MBA training had paid off for these luminaries of business. What they found was the exact opposite.

Ten out of the nineteen had significantly failed as CEOs of their organizations. What does this mean? Well, either their companies went bankrupt, they were removed as CEO, or there was some other major organizational failure. Sounds rough, huh? Well, there's more. According to their research, the success and tenure of four more were considered to be on shaky ground. The skills and training they had received from Harvard had gotten them in the door, but when they were faced with the struggles of day-to-day operations, they'd faltered.

So why did they fail? In many cases, it was valuing profit over people. One of the CEOs was specifically forced out because of a shady deal he'd made that would have cost his employees their jobs, over a couple of extra percentage points of return. In addition, these folks had been steeped in a culture that was old-fashioned and rigid—the business realm of twenty years ago.[5] They knew the right people to get them into the right jobs, but, faced with the task of managing real people, they were completely incompetent, costing them profit, position, and—perhaps the most valuable of these—people. While Harvard had given them plenty of case studies to prepare them for the purported real world, they were unable to succeed at handling the intricacies of the real humans they dealt with every day.

People don't leave bad jobs; they leave bad managers. Across Emplify's entire data set, the most common challenges we see are companies promoting top-performing employees into management and then leaving them to their own devices. Often, these new managers mean well. They're usually former high-performing line-level employees who have been promoted thanks to their hard work and tenure. Unfortunately, when they become managers, the business lacks the proper tools to help them succeed at leading their teams. The only thing these new managers have to fall back on is the outdated style of management. They're the kind of managers who become Frustrated Franks.

In an effort to lead their people, a Frank will bully their people into hitting performance goals. When a Frank thinks they are advising, they are actually chastising their staff, creating a huge divide between themselves and their people. As they feel this gap grow, a

---

5   Henry Mintzberg, "MBAs as CEOs: Some Troubling Evidence," Blog post, February 22, 2017, https://mintzberg.org/blog/mbas-as-ceos.

Frank will feel their control slipping and, in an effort to maintain it, buckle down even harder on their people. In order to look impressive at work, they'll hoard problems to themselves, unwilling to invite their people into tough problems. It's no wonder that the stereotypical boss you see in pop culture seems to have high blood pressure. They're putting an immense amount of stress on themselves, and only they can release it. What these Franks need is to take a step back from their role and understand what their own unique brand of leadership is. Oh, and they'll also need some practical skills—some of which you can find later in this book.

A manager's style is one of the most important aspects to running a successful organization. According to a study published by *Forbes*, a majority of employees would rather see their boss fired than receive a pay raise, citing dissatisfaction and lack of opportunity as the key drivers to this decision. What's more, people with bad managers take an average of fifteen more sick days than their counterparts do.[6] Bad leadership means disengaged and absent employees who are unmotivated and unproductive. Businesses can't afford to have a disruptive manager on the loose wreaking havoc on their team's productivity. The reign of these Frustrated Franks must come to an end!

> A majority of employees would rather see their boss fired than receive a pay raise.

In order to illustrate the damage that Franks can have on your people, I want to share a story about a job I had after I left Commonway Church. Cara and I had just had two boys, and we needed a way to support our growing family. So I started looking for

---

6   Meghan Casserly, "Majority of Americans Would Rather Fire Their Boss Than Get a Raise," *Forbes*, October 17, 2012, https://www.forbes.com/sites/meghancasserly/2012/10/17/majority-of-americans-would-rather-fire-their-boss-than-get-a-raise/#728b9a376610.

a job—just any job—and, at Cara's request, one with benefits. After a couple of submissions on Indeed, I found both, which, at the time, was a big win for us. The position was at a small university where the commute wouldn't be far from our home. The money was okay— enough to feed my growing family. It also doesn't take much when you're used to making a hundred dollars a week on a music leader's salary. When I first started, I was excited to begin a new phase of my life where I'd be providing more fully for my family.

Little did I know, however, that the job would be miserable. There was just nothing to do! Each day, I'd come in at 9:00 a.m. and do about ninety minutes of work. After that, I'd find ways to waste time until I could clock out. This wasn't for lack of trying, though. The leadership brought me on with no plan and only a slim idea of what the job should be. So instead of doing anything I'd consider to be work, I'd spend hours playing fantasy football or updating my Myspace page in an attempt to revive my music career. While I did amass thousands of followers, it was clear that this would not be my path. (If only I'd picked the right social network!) Regardless: I was bored to tears. My job felt completely meaningless, and no one seemed to mind that I was spending most of my time getting abso- lutely no work done.

My manager—a true Frank—didn't care that I was bored. Strangely, the only thing she did seem to care about was how many hours were on my time sheet at the end of the week. If I showed up to the office five minutes before her, I'd be praised all day for my dedication to my position. If I walked in a couple of minutes late, however, I was chastised for my poor performance. During my time working with her, I discovered that she was completely out of touch with who I was and what I needed to thrive. She had one of the core attributes of a Frank manager—she was focused on the hours I put in, and not the output of my work. She didn't care that a majority of those hours were spent memorizing all of the acceptable two- and three-letter words in Scrabble—a last-ditch attempt to best Cara at her own game.

What's worse, my manager was completely at ease in letting me rot in my ergonomic chair with lumbar support. While we had weekly touch-base meetings, I sensed no big ideas or vision coming from her in those sessions. In fact, she, like many other Frank managers, had no interest in the ideas of her staff or what they brought to the table. In her mind, she thought I was lucky to have the job I had. This was true of the original Frank who'd stopped my lecture too! These kinds of managers think their employees work for them, and they should do it with a smile. Unfortunately, this creates passionless teams who drag themselves into work every day to do the bare minimum. These kinds of dead-end jobs are torture for everyone. It's not a job—it's a prison.

Being a manager doesn't mean you need to be a monster. It's time to break free of the old Frank style and learn how to lead your own way. Understanding how you lead, however, can mean taking a long look in the mirror. Vincent Siciliano, CEO of the New Resource Bank, a small, independently run financial institution in California, came to understand this firsthand when he was brought on to turn the struggling bank around. While the first year of his tenure saw some success in his style, an organizational analysis showed that a majority of the staff were disengaged and displeased with his leadership. Engagement was low among lower-level employees and C-suite leadership alike, and many attributed this directly to Vince.

One of the biggest concerns was that Vince was just moving too fast for his people to keep up. He was pushing massive new practices on his staff without taking into account their role in enacting the changes that would come with them. Instead of wallowing in this terrible news, however, Vince put his ego aside and sat down with his staff to fix the problems that he had created. Within a couple of months, not only was morale better, but New Resource had several high-performing teams working to capture new leads in the market.[7] Vince's self-reflection and the use of objective data helped him understand what it meant to lead like a human.

Human-centric leaders share a couple of attributes that I think it's important you know about as you continue on your own journey of leadership. These kinds of leaders are authentic, collaborative, and able to cast a vision for their staff. Instead of considering their people as pawns to be ordered around, they see leading their people well as their personal responsibility and view the fact that they have been entrusted to lead as an honor. These kinds of leaders find a moral imperative in providing meaningful and engaging work for their people. As I've mentioned before, I've met and worked with many Franks in my lifetime, but finding a manager who leads like a human has been rare. One of the best managers I've worked for, and someone whom I consider a model for this behavior, was the manager at my first sales gig.

After about a year at the university (or, as my manager saw it, 2,080 working hours), I realized that I needed a new job. Once again, I submitted my résumé anywhere that had an open position to be filled. Before long, I was offered a sales position at SpinWeb, a web-development company. While I had never done sales, I was immediately attracted to the culture of the company and the team. They all seemed to be working incredibly hard and were still very, very happy at their jobs. From day one, I realized this was a direct

---

[7] Rasmus Hougaard, Jacqueline Carter, and Marissa Afton, "Self-Awareness Can Help Leaders More Than an MBA Can," *Harvard Business Review*, January 12, 2018, https://hbr.org/2018/01/self-awareness-can-help-leaders-more-than-an-mba-can.

result of the leadership of the CEO at SpinWeb—Michael Reynolds.

On my first day, Michael pulled me aside and told me something that has become essential to my own style of leadership. In the corner of this small office, he said to me, "I don't care when you work; I don't care how you work; I don't even care where you work. What I'm curious about is, if you really set your mind to unlocking this business, what are you capable of doing?" I'd never had a manager speak so honestly to me. I could feel he was being his authentic self, and, in his behavior, I found the permission to let down my own walls. So, when I finally heard a leader say, "I believe in you and what you can do," I put my whole self in. Michael had given me the exact push I needed, so I dedicated myself to mastering sales.

Frustrated Frank
My employees are lucky to be a part of my team and have a job at a successful company.

Human-Centric Leader
My employees have made the decision to work for me, and it's my responsibility to ensure their work is challenging and meaningful.

Michael's outcomes-first style of management was known as ROWE, which stands for "Results-Only Work Environment." I wasn't the only one taken with the approach. The entire team seemed on fire—ready and willing to do the work and grow the business. **What Michael was giving us was clarity of direction, belief in**

leadership, and freedom—everything you can expect from a human-centric leader. I had only just started learning sales, but I woke up every day motivated and excited that my work could have a direct impact my life and the business. Michael's belief and empowerment unlocked my potential. In my first year at SpinWeb, I had the best year of sales in company history. By my second year, I had nearly doubled the results from year one.

At SpinWeb, I was doing twice (if not three times) the work I did in my previous position. But in no way did I feel overworked or burned out. If anything, I felt the opposite—impassioned and invigorated. Michael let me know that my contributions mattered to the overall business and that I had a personal stake in the success of the company. He also knew that I wanted to learn more about sales, and he made it his personal mission to teach me everything he knew. At SpinWeb, I learned how a group of engaged, hardworking individuals can make a huge impact in the world, and how one person can motivate and encourage a team to take on anything.

Michael knew his staff on a deep and personal level. He cared for them, and in return they cared for him. His team worked harder and put in more hours because that two-way relationship was there. This is incredibly rare for a manager! The Franks of the world, for example, separate themselves from their staff through their management. Instead of creating a lasting relationship, they seek to make bonds with their employees that are only as good as the next paycheck. They lack purpose in their work and are unable to give their people the clarity of vision they need to do their work. Because of these things, their people leave for better opportunities and, with luck, better managers. So you have a choice: Do you want to be a Frank, constantly burdened by a disengaged and dwindling workforce? Or do you want to be like Michael and create a motivated and engaged team?

CHAPTER FOUR

WHAT IS EMPLOYEE ENGAGEMENT?

The product of the head, heart and hand is a thing to be loved.

—Elbert Hubbard

As I think back to my time at SpinWeb, I realize that Michael had a keen way of leading the team to accomplish great things. He was incredibly precise in the way he laid out his expectations for each of us and how we fit into creating SpinWeb's future. This clarity of purpose turned me and the rest of the team into productivity machines. When at the university, I would only work for about ninety minutes each day and then feel exhausted after that. At SpinWeb, I was on fire, putting in as much time as I could to get the job done. I stopped thinking about the work I did as a time commitment and instead was focused on achieving the goals Michael helped set for the company. I felt that I had the freedom to succeed, and it was up to me to seize the opportunity. At SpinWeb, we were all working toward a clearly defined goal, inspired by the vision of a leader who we knew had our backs.

In an ideal world, every team has a Michael leading them, and thus every team is made up of those highly motivated workers we had at SpinWeb. Unfortunately, that's not the case for most American businesses. Our research at Emplify shows that at least 70 percent of the workforce is currently disengaged at their jobs. This is a serious problem for businesses, costing the United States upward of $450 billion in lost productivity every year.[8] We've also seen that these disengaged folks will leave quickly when they feel their needs are not being met, again costing businesses time and resources in refilling their positions. These organizational problems, however, don't leave with the employee: it's just a "rinse and repeat" as more and more employees leave.

Much of this comes down to problems in leadership. As we discussed in the last chapter, many organizational issues can be directly traced back to poorly performing managers who are either undertrained or are following a management style that's inauthentic. The employees are simply not feeling supported or engaged by these kinds of leaders. Disengagement is wrecking our workforce today, and, in most cases, it's a top-down problem. But don't let that discourage you! As a leader, you have the power to root out the causes of disengagement before it becomes an active disruption to the organization as a whole. Disengaged employees lead to a lack of productivity in your staff which in turn lowers profits, increases turnover, stagnates innovation, and harms your overall brand reputation.

Impact of Disengagement

| disengaged workers | lower productivity | lack of innovation | lower profitability |

---

8   Susan Sorenson and Keri Garman, "How to Tackle US Employees' Stagnating Engagement," *Business Journal*, June 11, 2013.

Disengaged employees are like a cancer to the company: they will actively push your organization away from its mission and values. While engaged employees will use their discretionary time innovating, disengaged people will likely use any discretionary time they have to spread negativity or do counterproductive work, which ultimately lowers the performance of the whole team. This, in turn, causes more staff to become frustrated and underappreciated at work. Without real leadership, disengaged employees will just continue to spread their toxic behavior until it hamstrings your entire organization.

The negative attitude and demeanor of these disengaged employees can eat away at the productivity and innovation of your organization. They'll do the bare minimum to get by in their work, and if they aren't doing that, they might even be actively contributing to production failures. An engaged worker, on the other hand, can boost productivity and even empower innovations across your enterprise. According to a recent study from Bain Consulting, an engaged employee is 44 percent more productive than a satisfied employee.[9] Engagement is directly linked to how your people do their work every day and come up with great new ideas while they're on the job. And while disengaged employees are indeed disrupting your organization, the disruption isn't happening in the way you want.

The final thing at risk in a disengaged workforce is your reputation. Remember how, because of today's social job-searching platforms, employees can now rate and review their jobs while they're on the job? Think about the kind of review a disengaged employee will leave on your organization's Glassdoor page. Other job seekers take those reviews seriously. Just one bad review could be the deciding

---

9   Stephanie Vozza, "Why Employees at Apple and Google Are More Productive," *Fast Company*, March 13, 2017, https://www.fastcompany.com/3068771/how-employees-at-apple-and-google-are-more-productive.

factor on whether or not someone puts in a résumé for your most recent open position. Now imagine if thousands of disengaged employees got the word out about how poorly your company is run, or what a bad place it is to work. Your current talent pipeline could drop to nil. Seventy-five percent of Americans said they wouldn't be willing to work for a company with a bad reputation—even if they were currently unemployed.[10] If businesses want the best and brightest talent, they need to first focus on the people they already have working for them.

> Seventy-five percent of Americans said they wouldn't be willing to work for a company with a bad reputation—even if they were currently unemployed.

It might be obvious that a disengaged employee will have many negative impacts on your company and its operations. But there is another type of employee who is also adversely affecting your bottom line in a subtler and more indirect way. These are satisfied employees whose attitudes sit in the middle of disengaged and engaged. A satisfied employee is the kind of person who's mired in the old way of thinking about work. They think only about how the work they do each day relates to their paycheck at the end of the month.

This attitude is primarily due to how managers used to track satisfaction among their employees twenty years ago. Leadership would conduct surveys asking employees three questions about their current positions: Are you comfortable at your job? Have you considered quitting? And will you refer your friends to this company? Based on the responses, they measured how purportedly satisfied their

---

10   Glassdoor Team, "Why a Company's Reputation Matters, Even in a Bad Economy," Glassdoor, October 3, 2012, https://www.glassdoor.com/blog/companys-reputation-matters-bad-economy/.

employees were, and they then used that data to make strategic HR decisions. Unfortunately, due to insufficient data-gathering methods and faulty ways of thinking, this survey for satisfaction completely ignored the other factors that go into how people feel about their jobs. They just had no way of measuring a person's level of engagement! This led to a culture of satisfaction in which employees clocked in and clocked out without any thought to what their work could be or the potential that lay dormant within them. Meanwhile, executives focused on satisfaction-motivation tactics like benefits and perks. **On the surface, these satisfied people might seem like they're hard workers who are on the right path, but don't let them fool you!**

Satisfaction Is Good	Engagement Is Great
Am I comfortable and am I going to stay?	How can I drive the business forward?
I work only enough to meet basic expectations.	My heart and mind are in it and I give 115% every day.

So, what are the warning signs of a satisfied employee? Their body language might be a first tell. At the office, satisfied folks are leaning back because they haven't been called on to step up. Leadership hasn't given much thought to what can motivate them to do better and, instead, settles for meeting expectations. Satisfied employees are happy with their compensation and benefits and how those things are balanced with the amount of work they're doing each day. For the most part, they don't feel inspired or committed to do great work. Overall, they're comfortable at work, so they won't try to put up roadblocks like a disengaged employee might. As long as a paycheck is coming in, they're not thinking about leaving the organization anytime soon. To them, they think that they've landed a cushy gig where they can just coast, doing little to no work and collecting all the benefits and pay they want.

And, of course, they will recommend the job to a friend or colleague! If they feel like they're getting a sweet deal with little to no effort, they'll put in recommendations for all their friends, attracting more people who just want the pay with no real progress or passion. But the moment they find a new opportunity with better salary, compensation, or perks, they'll put in their notice, leaving you with a gap in your team that will need to be filled. Just as a disengaged employee can detract from your more engaged people, a satisfied employee hinders you from creating an engaged culture.

So far, we know what engagement is not. It's not disengagement, where apathetic employees actively work against your organization. It's also not satisfaction, where competent but complacent workers do the bare minimum. **Engagement, as we at Emplify define it, is an employee's intellectual (head) and emotional (heart) connection with an employer, demonstrated by motivation and commitment (hands) to have a positive impact on the company's vision and goals.** It's how employees think about their jobs in their heads and feel about their employers in their hearts, and how those two things manifest in their day-to-day work.

At an organizational level, engagement is an energy and motivation in the workforce that's caused by real investments made by leadership. As with everything, engagement is a spectrum—it's almost impossible for a certain individual or team to be consistently 100 percent engaged at all times. Although it is certainly my goal! And why not set a lofty goal to achieve as a leader? It's your job to work toward creating a highly engaged environment where the vast majority of your people will be engaged. An engaged workforce turns the tides on all the problems brought on by satisfied and disengaged folks. This kind of workforce creates a surge in productivity in staff, which in turn increases profits, reduces turnover, catalyzes innovation, and creates a workforce of brand evangelists for your organization.

Engagement is a lean-forward attitude that shows employees' passion for what they do. Engaged employees have a higher level of focus at work and a higher pace of work, and they feel good about the work they do. Engaged employees come in every day ready to take on the company's purpose and put in the extra effort in their day-to-day work. They have a clear understanding of what their role is and how it fits into the larger strategy of the organization. They are motivated to drive the business forward however they can because they have a personal stake in the success of the company. This drive causes them to spend precious discretionary effort—hours spent after major business tasks are completed—to help figure out more advanced problems related to your clients and your company. Every day, these folks bring their whole selves to work and are constantly asking themselves how they can do more for their team and their company.

An engaged employee's commitment also translates to job tenure. These kinds of employees have been shown to be 87 percent less likely to leave than their satisfied peers.[11] And when an entire company is populated by engaged and excited employees, your company can expect big returns. According to Gallup, in 2018 organizations with higher levels of employee engagement saw more customer loyalty, an overall increase in sales, and a 21 percent increase in profit.[12] Another Gallup study showed that engagement isn't only about increasing profits; it's also about boosting innovation. The majority of engaged employees (59 percent) who were a part of this study said that their jobs brought out "their most creative ideas," compared to just 3 percent of employees who were disengaged.[13] An engaged workforce is, without a doubt, a harder-working and more inspiring group for this new age of business. Creating and keeping this kind of engaged culture is key for companies that want to stay ahead. But before I go through the practical steps to leading like a human and how to build high-performance teams in this new era, let's explore how to encourage engagement in your own organization.

Several discrete factors dictate whether or not employees are engaged and willing to bring their best selves to work. Humans are complicated creatures, and these factors range from interpersonal issues to larger infrastructural alignments. Our research has shown that seventeen different drivers are responsible for employee engagement:

---

11   Elizabeth Kiehner, "What You Risk by Forgetting Employee Engagement," *Inc.*, April 23, 2018, https://www.inc.com/elizabeth-kiehner/whats-forgotten-in-cultures-and-your-companys-obsession-with-technology.html.

12   Jim Harter, "Employee Engagement on the Rise in the US," Gallup, August 26, 2018, https://news.gallup.com/poll/241649/employee-engagement-rise.aspx.

13   Jerry Krueger and Emily Killham, "The Innovation Equation," Gallup, April 12, 2007, https://news.gallup.com/businessjournal/27145/innovation-equation.aspx.

AUTONOMY
A measure of the organizational culture. The organization trusts employees to use their expertise to make decisions about how to do their jobs.

 LEADER AVAILABILITY
A measure of the organization's leadership. Leaders are approachable, visible, accessible, and readily available to all employees in the organization.

 PURPOSE
A measure of the organizational culture. The organization communicates to employees why it exists beyond making a profit.

 CAPACITY
A measure of the organizational culture. The organization enables employees to feel they possess the emotional and psychological resources necessary for investing themselves in their roles.

 LEADER INTEGRITY
A measure of the organization's leadership. Employees see leaders as committed to doing what is best for them, and as able to follow through on that commitment.

 REST
A measure of the organizational culture. The organization gives employees a sense that they can take time off when needed.

 COWORKER RELATIONS
A measure of an employee's relationship with their coworkers. There are amicable interactions among coworkers leading to positive relationships at the organization.

 MANAGER
A measure of an employee's direct manager. The relationship between the employee and their manager that looks at respect, fairness, and development.

 ROLE CLARITY
A measure of the organizational culture. The organization connects employees' daily work tasks to the purpose of the business and provides clarity about what that work is.

 FAIRNESS
A measure of the organization's leadership. Leaders help employees feel that the rewards and treatment of individuals are fair within the organization.

 MEANING
A measure of the organizational culture. The organization helps employees have a sense of value (purpose, money, status, and influence) when they immerse themselves in their roles.

 SHARED VALUES
A measure of an employee's relationship with their coworkers. Coworkers share common work attitudes.

 FEEDBACK
A measure of the employee's direct manager. Employees feel that they receive adequate and helpful feedback from their manager.

 PROFESSIONAL DEVELOPMENT
A measure of the organizational culture. The organization promotes and encourages employees' professional development.

 UTILIZATION
A measure of the organizational culture. The organization effectively uses employees' abilities and skills in their roles.

 GOAL SUPPORT
A measure of the organizational culture. The organization makes efforts to remove structural barriers that prevent an employee from achieving their goals.

 PSYCHOLOGICAL SAFETY
A measure of an employee's direct manager. Individuals have the sense that they can show and employ their true selves at work without fear of negative consequences to self-image, status, or career.

EMPLOYEE ENGAGEMENT DRIVERS

Each of these drivers works in tandem with the others to provide a road map for leaders who wish to foster engagement in their organizations. While every company will have its own set of unique issues, these seventeen drivers account for a majority of the root causes of disengaged cultures. And not all of these drivers are created equal, either. Based on your organization's specific attributes, some drivers will have a bigger influence than others. Identifying what the key drivers are in your organization is the first step to creating and keeping a highly engaged culture.

At the beginning of this chapter, I mentioned that disengaged employees are like a sickness that can easily spread throughout your company. The good news is that the same can be said of engaged employees. Their attitude and hard work will bring up everyone around them, creating a harmonious workforce that is in lockstep with your company's vision and values. It only takes one person to create the change you're looking for, and that person is you. It's why, as a leader, it's important that you know how you show up to work every day and how that affects the way you lead.

Throughout these first four chapters, I've shared with you my own experience and perspective on leadership and business. I've done this so I could illustrate what I think are the most pressing issues facing industries today, and how a simple change in thinking can radically improve both the bottom line of the business and the well-being of your people. In the pursuit of my own mission to unlock the best in people, I've let you in on my wandering journey from pastor to entrepreneur and have shared anecdotes that I hope you will find valuable on your own path. Now that you've decided you're committed to this journey toward a new style of leadership, which I hope you have, let's talk about some practical skills you'll need in leading like a human. In the next six chapters, I'll be giving you tactical tips for unlocking the potential in your people and creating the type of highly engaged teams that achieve unprecedented results. If you bring the whole energy of yourself to setting these things into practice, you'll have everything you need to become the type of leader you've always envisioned yourself to be. What's more, you'll create the kinds of teams who are achieving performance goals you couldn't have imagined. And the first step toward this starts with you. Are you ready?

CHAPTER FIVE

STEP ONE: CENTEREDNESS

Gradually, you will return to yourself,
Having learned a new respect for your heart
And the joy that dwells far within slow time.

—John O'Donohue

Now, if you're not committed to taking on the task of becoming the leader you were meant to be, I understand. You can close the book right here, put it back on the shelf of your office, and leave it there until, eventually, you donate it to Goodwill, where it'll find good company among the CDs I produced during my music career. But, if what I've shared has resonated with you, if what you've read has stirred in you a desire to grow an engaged culture, if you're committed to starting this new journey toward leading like a human, if you want to rid yourself of the Frustrated Frank who lives inside of you, then it is of the utmost importance that you take to heart what I've put down in this chapter. The skills and lessons you'll find here are something I believe in fervently because I have seen the difference they've made—both in myself and in other leaders. It's in finding a personal centeredness where you will also discover the foundation for leading like a human. To lead in this new way, you need to be committed to the journey and keep yourself balanced while you're on it—even in the toughest times.

Now, perhaps you want to skip ahead, thinking: *I know how to keep myself centered! I just need the tactical skills to get my people motivated.* This way of thinking, however, is deeply flawed. Look, people today are seeking leaders who can be confident in themselves and rise above the noise to give them direction. Studies have shown that employees' perception of an authentic leader is the single biggest predictor for whether or not they are happy at their jobs.[14] The keyword here is *authentic*—people who are willing and able to be themselves. This chapter is about finding that authenticity in yourself, and how to keep it at work. If you can't do that, then the tactics in the rest of this book will come off as hollow. You'll be doing the work, but you'll become frustrated—not unlike those Franks we mentioned earlier. These tips just won't work if you're not an authentic leader who has committed yourself to this best version of you.

One thing I have found that separates a Frank-type leader from a human-centric Michael-style leader is how they perceive time. Time, in many situations, is our most valuable resource, and it's best not to waste it. Frank-type leaders, however, never think they have enough of it and, in an effort to fill their days, take on more and more projects until they feel overworked and

> Time, in many situations, is our most valuable resource, and it's best not to waste it.

---

14 Susan Jensen and Fred Luthans, "Entrepreneurs as Authentic Leaders: Impact on Employees' Attitudes," *Leadership and Organizational Development Journal*, December 2006.

exhausted. They're so overly focused on the things they need to accomplish in that day, that hour, or that thirty-minute slot, that they miss the big opportunities for radical innovation. These Frank leaders are incapable of escaping the tyranny of the current moment. You can't be above a problem when you are in a problem.

Human-centric leaders, in contrast, are able to see beyond what's happening in the here and now and envision a successful future. They bring this perspective to their organization and are able to see that there are some things that take priority over their job. They know that to be the best leader they can be, they need to take the time to ask themselves, "What do I, as a person, need right now?" In order to find centeredness in the storm that is everyday life, human-centric leaders craft daily practices that still their thoughts and help them make decisions that will have an impact on future goals.

Each individual's practice is unique to their own lifestyle, but what I have found is that they each begin with coming to know themselves deeply. After they have set this into practice, they create other daily habits such as caring for their mind and body and finding a hobby to keep themselves grounded. As you create your own routine, you will gain centeredness and confidence that will then help you transform your style of leadership. Making the time to look inward is the first step in creating your practice and will illuminate how you can become your own kind of leader—no Frank or Michael needed.

CREATE A DAILY PRACTICE OF SELF-REFLECTION

A practice means it is something you do every day. Before you create your daily practice, you need to spend some time with yourself in quiet self-reflection. Are you doing what feels the most fulfilling or what you feel you were meant to do? Are you leading in a way that reflects your values? Ask yourself honestly: What are the things that are blocking me from becoming that person? Taking a long hard look in the mirror might be painful, but it's an essential step toward unlocking your own great potential. When you've answered these questions about yourself, it's important to make self-reflection a part of your daily practice. Naming your feelings as they come up is a great way to understand how you show up as a leader. If you can't name your feelings, then you won't be able to do the work necessary to address them.

A great place to do all of this self-reflection is in a journal or some other kind of record that contains your intentions, self-reflections, and priorities. I first learned my method of journaling from Reboot, a coaching company that helped me in my own leadership journey. I've learned firsthand how important journaling can be as I've grown as a leader. If you're stuck with what to put in your journal, ask yourself some of the following questions that my coach gave me when I first started journaling:

- What are you noticing about yourself today?

- How are you showing up at work and in your personal life?

- What is bringing you energy today?

- What is causing you stress?

In keeping this journal, you'll be able to quiet your other hectic thoughts and listen to the quiet voice that speaks deep in your heart. These quiet moments of looking inward will help you understand what's happening inside and how it affects your behavior. They will give you an inner touchpoint to return to.

FIND YOUR PLACE IN IT ALL

Another part of this practice is taking the time to look out and **root yourself in something larger** than your person and your current situation. This prevents that "tyranny of the moment" that I talked about earlier. It can be a spiritual practice that feels appropriate to you, such as praying, meditating, or reading something timelessly true. It can be engaging in some form of art or culture, or even nature. Whatever it is, it's meant to give you a broader perspective than your own. One great way to do this is to read a book of poetry or a novel. Reading can make you more available to the causes and concerns of others. It has the power to take you out of your own experience and imagine new stories, new people, and new ideas.

This imagination, in turn, makes you more empathetic. A study examining how fiction affects our cognitive function found that the way our brains process fictional stories and the way they process real events is identical, which basically means that hearing stories helps you understand another person's circumstances better. People who read are working this empathy muscle every time they pick up a book.[15] By making this part of your practice, you're able to understand that some things are much bigger than you and practice how you process and show empathy.

And let's face it, getting leaders to read is challenging! My book is probably the umpteenth one about work you've picked up today. I know because I, too, have voraciously consumed business books en masse, trying to crack the code on creative contingency planning or how to uncover the secrets behind improved synergistic collaboration. I'm sorry to say there is no ultimate answer in these books,

---

15 Society for Personality and Social Psychology, "Can Fiction Stories Make Us More Empathetic?" Public release, August 11, 2014, https://www.eurekalert.org/pub_releases/2014-08/sfpa-cfs081114.php.

or my own, that will instantly make you some insanely successful business wizard. But you know where you will find a bit of magic? The *Harry Potter* series.

GET YOURSELF A HOBBY

When you're consumed with the day-to-day, it's hard to let work do anything but exhaust you. You need to do something with your hands that isn't related at all to your job. Naming your hobbies helps you stay centered and grounded and is a great addition to your daily practice. I first realized this after my family had come back from a vacation. We were flipping through pictures, and I saw that I looked horrible—tired and fifteen pounds heavier. Santiago and I were working nonstop starting our first company, and I had let it consume me. The stress wasn't only affecting my physical appearance—it began to affect my inner self too. I was having outbursts at work. I wasn't as present with my kids as I like to be. It dawned on me that what I needed was something to do outside of my work: I needed a hobby.

So, I bought three chickens, put them in my backyard, and tended to them as if they were my own little egg farm. Every day, I'd feed them, water them, clean their cages, and, every day, I'd get an egg from each of them. While it might seem silly, seeing my hard work pay off was a huge stress reliever. I found myself more present at home and more grounded when facing stressful situations as work. It was incredible to see that what I did with my hands made a real impact on something outside of myself and my worries at work. It gives you a sense of purpose, and also a sense of time. Now, I'm not telling everyone to go out and get chickens. Your hobby could be anything that gives you a sense of accomplishment. Playing an instrument, baking bread, or gardening are all possibilities, and good ones at that.

FOCUS ON YOUR HEALTH

Lastly, you must spend some time **taking care of your physical health**. That was another big takeaway from looking at those pictures of stressed and worn-down Adam. Even getting in a walk around the block or just being outside in nature will be incredibly beneficial—anything that gets your body active will have a tremendous impact. It has been proven that any amount of regular exercise gives you the energy you need to get through the workday with confidence and groundedness.[16]

LEARN TO MAKE THIS YOUR OWN

After you have all these pieces in your practice—**a method for self-reflection, a way to root yourself in something larger, a hobby outside of work, and a way to be physical**—keep a healthy schedule that will help you to stick to this new routine and order. By keeping to this daily practice, you'll continue to show up consistently as a growing and empathetic leader. Make the time and space for each of these important parts of your day.

The hard truth is that there is no magic bullet to becoming an "authentic leader." It's a combination of doing the work to become an "authentic person" and applying solid leadership principles and tactics. People who get to know themselves deeply—understanding their

> The hard truth is that there is no magic bullet to becoming an "authentic leader." It's a combination of doing the work to become an "authentic person" and applying solid leadership principles and tactics.

---

16 "Exercise: Seven Benefits of Regular Physical Activity," Mayo Clinic, May 11, 2019, https://www.mayoclinic.org/healthy-lifestyle/fitness/in-depth/exercise/art-20048389.

strengths and weaknesses—can observe what triggers them and can navigate how they can control those triggers. As they grow in this journey, they can learn to name different aspects of who they are and how those things affect others who surround them. Authentic leaders are those who are physically and mentally healthy and lead their lives with intentionality—rather than just drifting. That is literally what it means to be a leader—you have to lead. Even if that means going against the current.

While each of you will create your own routine, I want to share with you mine in the hope that it might give you some ideas for your own practice. First, I never sleep with my phone beside the bed. I do this so I'm not tempted to check emails or do any work first thing in the morning. Instead, first thing in the morning I read some poetry or something that is timelessly true. Right now, I'm reading a book of John O'Donohue's poetry entitled *To Bless the Space Between Us*. After that, I work out for thirty minutes. What I do varies each day, and I don't stress about having the perfect workout; I just make sure I dedicate thirty minutes every day to my physical health. Finally, I always take at least three minutes to intentionally practice gratitude. This typically happens after I drop my kids off at school on my walk home (sometimes it happens during a silent commute to the office), but practically what I do is take the time to think about all the things I'm grateful for in incredible detail—my wife Cara, my kids, air-conditioning, that one time I beat Cara at Scrabble, food, shelter, clean water, you name it! Nothing is too insignificant—what's important is that I have a dedicated time to focus on what I'm grateful for. Before beginning work, I take a deep breath and remind myself that my team needs an authentic and centered leader today. After that, I exhale, open my car door, and calmly walk into the office.

Now, this isn't a how-to guide or a book on the benefits of waking up early. In fact, I have plenty of colleagues where early to bed and early to rise make them nothing but grumpy and exhausted. We are all different people with different sleep patterns and rhythms. Again, there's no magic bullet or universal answer to what inspires and grounds us. But what I'm asking is that you think about what centers you with intention and care. Take this moment to ask yourself the following questions: "What adjustments do I need to make in my life to grow in my self-awareness?" "What do I need in my day-to-day to help myself become more centered?" When you've answered these questions, you'll be able to approach the coming work stressors with a steady confidence that will instill trust and belief in others. This is your strong foundation of leading like a human.

By creating this practice, you give yourself a stable ground to stand on so that your employees can look to you and sense your calm, steadying presence. A centered leader is a person who leads like a human—with authenticity, vulnerability, and purpose. That behavior won't only calm your people; it'll excite and invigorate them too. Together, you'll be able to rally around the work you do every day, inspired by a purpose that everyone can see themselves in.

ACTIVATE IT!

Hello, hello! Thanks for joining me in our "Activate It!" section, where you will find ways to take actionable steps in turning what I've shared with you into something real and tangible. As I mentioned before, these steps will fall flat if you don't make what you've read here into something you live out each and every day. This section is meant to be your working guide where you'll find questions and definitions to help you on your journey toward leading the way you were always meant to lead.

DEFINE IT

Practice is a daily structure that includes habits to help you find centeredness in your everyday routine.

- Set aside a time of the day focused on quiet self-contemplation to meditate on your intentions, passions, and emotions.

- Create a list of daily rituals that will give you structure for the day and help center you in yourself. Make sure in this daily practice that you include the following:

    - a way to root yourself in something bigger than yourself;

    - a physical activity that gets your blood pumping;

    - a hobby that you work at that has nothing to do with your job.

- Stick to this practice in a way that feels authentic to you. You should be able to scale it to adjust to the scheduling needs of the day.

LIVE IT OUT

- Journaling is a great way to archive your moments of self-reflection in order to track your progress and better understand yourself.

- Physical activity should suit you. Find an exercise plan that works for your body and your level of comfort.

- Hobbies should help you see the result of the work you put into them. Track your progress during your moments of self-reflection.

- Pausing for moments of gratitude throughout your day gives you purpose as you go about your daily tasks.

MAKE IT YOURS

- What things make you feel centered, and how can you incorporate them into your daily routine?

- What's a physical activity that you enjoy and that you could see yourself continuing to do?

- What are your hobbies?

- What are you grateful for each day?

- How can you support your team on their journey to become more centered?

ACTIVATE IT! NOTES

_____

_____

_____

_____

_____

_____

_____

_____

_____

_____

_____

_____

_____

_____

_____

_____

_____

_____

_____

_____

_____

CHAPTER SIX

STEP TWO: ALIGN AROUND YOUR COMPANY PURPOSE

The purpose answers the ageless question: "Why?" Why does what we do matter and what difference are we making in the world?

—Verne Harnish, *Scaling Up*

Back in the nineties, there were these popular inspirational posters that seemed to hang in every office. They always depicted something like an eagle or a mountain surrounded by a black border with a word in big block type—**PERSEVERANCE** or **EXCELLENCE**—and below that, an even quippier aspirational phrase. I'm not sure where these pictures came from or why they were hung up, but I can guess that it was some attempt to inspire employees who were crammed in cubicles and banging out meaningless reports. As the years went on, these posters gathered dust as they simply blended into the scenery of the workplace. The people they were meant to inspire ignored the words and ideas held behind the dusty glass of the frame and instead focused on when they could clock out next. What was meant to be a powerful illustrator of culture fell flat, only to become a hollow stand-in for a company's purpose.

While the days of these posters might have passed, the bankrupt attempt to infuse culture into organizations has not. Companies today are constantly looking for that quick fix to bring in new talent or attract new clients. Offering everything from snack jars to draft beer, these companies pursue new trends that they think will appeal to their people. As we've seen in chapters past, these perks are only satisfaction tactics and won't inspire the best in your people. If they aren't rooted in a strong culture, they will come off as hollow and inauthentic, causing more problems than solutions. Without a strong purpose-driven culture, leaders simply spin their wheels, rolling out one quick fix after another without ever truly tapping into the power of engagement.

> Companies today are constantly looking for that quick fix to bring in new talent or attract new clients. Offering everything from snack jars to draft beer, these companies pursue new trends that they think will appeal to their people.

Culture is not something you can create overnight. It doesn't come from a poster you can buy at a store or the Ping-Pong table in the breakroom. It comes from your people. Many of you reading this book might already have a purpose statement that you spent a lot of money hiring a branding agency to help you make a pithy sentence that ties together the vast offerings of your company. But is it inspiring to your people? And is it an active part of your culture that your organization lives out every day? As I mentioned in a previous chapter, the modern workforce truly values an activated purpose in choosing employment. They cite it as one of their top three priorities, in fact. In creating a clear and energizing purpose that inspires your people, you will take another step toward creating the culture of engagement that is so desperately needed in today's workforce. Once you've done that, you need to activate the purpose and make it real for your people.

WHAT MAKES A PURPOSE?

Let's start with what makes a purpose. A purpose statement is a clear and unique statement that powerfully answers the fundamental question: Why does your organization do what it does? Many business leaders, when asked what their company purpose is, will recite back their brand promise, an important statement that describes the overlap between a company's offerings and a customer's desire. This statement, while useful, completely ignores the employees and their work and instead puts the emphasis on the customer. While a promise is an offering to a customer, a purpose statement is a declaration of what your organization can do for the world that's different from any other company out there. It's something your people can believe in and, if used properly, can encourage engagement across an organization.

Remember that engagement is about the head, heart, and hands of your people. We've seen that people work hard when they have a clear directive from their leadership. A company's purpose is that directive at a much larger scale. It's a rallying cry to your people, inciting them to take action. It should feel natural to your people—almost like the words are already a part of their daily vernacular. A clear purpose ignites the heart and inspires the head so the hands can get to the work. Your company's purpose, if well articulated and created, becomes a mantra for your employees that will differentiate your organization from every other company.

Your purpose should feel unique to your organization and the people who work inside it. In order to find this purpose, you will need to dig deep into your company and its operations. I think of this like an archaeological survey where you are trying to discover the root of your organization and how it has become what it is today. In an effort to help them clear away some of the excavation dust, I help large groups of CEOs and founders work on creating their purpose together. On the surface, many of these folks have similar products or services, but maybe within different industries. When I ask them to tell me what they do, they recite that brand promise and say how they help their customer. When I ask them why they do what they do, they're a little more stumped.

To find your purpose, you must first answer the question, "Why?" Picture yourself describing your business to a five-year-old. If this was me, I'd describe what my company does: "Well, I lead a company that helps leaders use data to take the best actions to help their people." That five-year-old (and maybe even their parents) will probably blink at me and then say, "Why?" "Well," I might say, "because people are very complex, and leaders need data to help understand how to lead them." Again, the five-year-old will ask, "Why?" and then, "Why?" again, and then—well, you get the picture. The five-year-old will just keep asking why until I get to a simple and significant statement that they can understand. In those purpose-discovery sessions I mentioned earlier, I am that five-year-old, and I use this interrogatory technique to dive deep into the existence and purpose of a company. It's called the "five whys," and it was originally used at Toyota as a way to get to the bottom of an issue. When used to discover your purpose, it helps you excavate the unique meaning that lies beneath your organization.

While many companies might have similar offerings, no two

organizations are the same. Take Pepsi and Coca-Cola for example. Here we have a classic example of two companies that, on the surface, have the exact same offering: a sweet carbonated beverage. Their offerings are so similar that you could probably swap one product for the other, and you wouldn't be able to tell them apart—unless you're one of the maybe 5 percent of people who definitely can. I mean, how many times have you heard, "Is Pepsi okay?" when you've asked for a Coke at a restaurant? Despite their similarities, however, their purposes are vastly different. Coca-Cola, according to the company's website, proclaims that its purpose is to "refresh the world," whereas Pepsi's is to "create joyful moments." These two statements differentiate these companies from each other, and if you think about the ways they portray themselves in the market, you can see how their expression aligns with their purpose. While neither is better than the other (contentious words, I know), each of these companies has created a purpose that is unique to its view of the world.

When your purpose is clear and unique, it gives your people a direction to follow. It helps them know why they're doing what they're doing. It should be aspirational in a way that captures employees' hearts yet simple enough that they can wrap their heads around it to know how it affects the work they do with their hands. When you've done that, you've created a purpose that energizes your people. This also creates a real sweet spot for productivity. Studies have shown that when a purpose ignites employees' hearts and inspires their minds, employees are willing to give up to 40 percent of their discretionary time to their company.[17] When that happens, you've got a company culture that's engaged and motivated to accomplish a clear and lofty mission.

---

17   Verne Harnish, *Scaling Up* (Gazelles Inc. 2014), 97.

CREATING A PURPOSE STATEMENT

If you want an engaged workforce, you must first have a purpose that is tangible for your people. In order to do so, gather a group of individuals at your organization whom you feel have a vested interest in the organization and its success. You do this so you can create a purpose that feels authentically owned by the people of the company. Ask your team to write down their answers to questions like the following:

- What does our company do, and why?

- What makes the work we do important?

- What makes you get out of bed in the morning?

- What problems are we solving in the world?

- What does our company do that makes this real? Where is the impact?

Make sure these individuals write down their answers to the questions. Jotting something down physicalizes the answers and, in a way, makes them more tangible. In these answers, you're also beginning to create a vocabulary for your organization. Once you have all the sheets, pass them around to each other and read them out loud. Now, spend some time together digesting these answers. What is the commonality between them all? Where are the connections? This could take hours, and it could take days, but eventually, you will come to a consensus that will feel authentic and clear to you and the people you're representing.

After you've done this, you'll have a purpose statement. A sentence, however, is just a collection of words if there is no action behind it. A surefire way to spread disengagement is to create a purpose statement that has no bearing on the lives of your people. At that point, you might as well buy one of those inspirational posters, hang it up, and wait for the dust to accumulate, because that's what you've got. In order to activate your purpose, you need to integrate it into the daily lives of your people. Let me give you a couple of tips to activate your purpose so that it will feel real to you and to your people.

CONNECT YOUR PEOPLE TO YOUR PURPOSE

Your purpose is meaningless if your people never hear it. After you've taken the time to home in on a purpose statement, make sure you **connect your people to your new company purpose**. Create an effective communication strategy that tells your people what your company's purpose is and how it relates to the work they're doing every day. In your communications, use language that fits with your purpose so that your people can see its full expression. Some of this language can come from the words and images you devised with your "purpose team" in your previous sessions. This purpose team could also be helpful in supporting the work they created as they go about their interactions with the broader team. If you have the resources, I'd also suggest that you create a group or committee whose sole mission is to spread your purpose throughout your organization and collect client stories that illustrate your purpose in action.

But spreading your purpose is not just a marketing exercise. Your purpose is also a way to lead and inspire your people. Managers can use a clear purpose statement to create the goals and set the priorities for their team. They can also use your purpose to help employees see how even mundane tasks still make a big impact on the company's purpose. Good purpose statements should also clearly lay out a direction for the organization so that individual employees can understand the big movements of the business and where they can push those movements forward. When writing job descriptions, make sure your company's purpose is clearly outlined and that it is tied back to the open position you're seeking. As we've seen in the past couple of chapters, your people are more engaged when they have a clear goal they're working toward. Linking those roles, goals, and objectives back to the company's purpose will help them understand that what they're working on has meaning and will encourage them to bring their best self every day.

A great example of this is a story about a janitor who was mopping the floors at NASA in 1962, during the infancy of the famous space agency. President John F. Kennedy was walking the halls, doing an inspection of the facilities, and stopped to ask the gentleman what he was doing. The janitor looked up at him and said, "Mr. President, I'm helping to put a man on the moon." This story has been used for decades to illustrate a lower-level employee's commitment to their role within a company. The way I see it, however, is that it shows how if a purpose is clearly defined, it can help employees find true impact in their work. While this man was just cleaning the floors, NASA's purpose helped him connect his role to the larger mission of the organization. When you connect your people to your purpose, they'll know that their work is valuable and that doing work inspired by your company's purpose can only result in success.

STORIES OF SUCCESS

A purpose statement is the baseline for what success looks like at an organization. Plain and simple. When your people understand where they've succeeded in that mission, they'll become even more engaged in their work. Sharing these stories of success will help your people understand what an activated purpose looks like and will encourage them to become engaged with the purpose as well.

Some of your folks might be working directly with your purpose every day, and others might be more removed from it. Your purpose might not be apparent to some sectors of your workforce, and that's okay. For that reason, **you have to have a system for saving success stories and sharing them across the entire organization**. This is where your team from the previous section comes in. **Create a cadence of story sharing where your employees can see your company's purpose in action**. As always, do this in a way that feels authentic to you and your organization. To combat that feeling of disengagement, bring the employees who are working closest to your company's purpose to teams that might seem more distant in order to bridge the gap.

At Emplify, our customer-facing team regularly meets with our more internal teams to share at least two stories of success to demonstrate to them how their work has impact—even if it's just in a supporting role. Every quarter, we hold an all-hands meeting where teams who have hit big milestones tell the rest of the company about the work they're doing and how it's moving our purpose forward. Lastly, as much as possible, **we try to get our customers into the building to meet our staff and share their stories themselves**. A story is best when it's coming from the horse's mouth. As I mentioned before, your purpose should help illustrate specific goals and objectives for your team. When they achieve those goals, celebrating those achievements helps reinforce your purpose to your people and in your culture. People also like to work with organizations that stand for something: incorporating customers is not only a best

> People also like to work with organizations that stand for something: incorporating customers is not only a best practice for your employees but also strengthens your relationship with your buyers.

practice for your employees but also strengthens your relationship with your buyers.

CELEBRATE MILESTONES

Your purpose should set the bar for everyone at your company—employee and executive alike. Every single one of your employees has the power to achieve big things for your company. When you've connected their work to the organization's purpose, you're sure to find folks who are pushing your organization forward in a big way. Maybe it's not an individual, but a team who has just accomplished something big. Whoever it is, help them understand how their achievement is not only a win for them, but for the whole company as well. Celebrate those milestones with your team so that they can feel energized by their work and their success and give the rest of the organization a model to aspire to.

A couple of years ago, a salesperson named Chip on our team had just sold his millionth dollar of new business, and we were celebrating his achievement in our office. For many small businesses, it takes years before they hit a million dollars in revenue, but here we had a guy who'd done it early on at our company, in a single fiscal year. We were all giving speeches about his career successes, sales expertise, outgoing personality, and cultural contributions. We hold these kinds of celebrations whenever we hit a company milestone, such as our first hundred thousand employees surveyed. We do this because it's important to recognize big milestones when they've been achieved. After listening to all the kind words, Chip stood up and said, "I am honored that all of you are here to celebrate me. I'm obviously thrilled with how the year has gone, and I couldn't have done it without all of you.

"I've been looking at the results over and over, and there was one thing that really shocked me. While we celebrate the amount of money I've sold, what's more important is how those sales have had a real impact on people across the country. I've done the numbers, and I've found that that million dollars represents well over forty-six thousand employee lives impacted because of the sales I've made. That means over forty thousand employees have had the opportunity to realize their true potential at work. For me, that's the greatest success I could've hoped for, and it's inspiring to me to see my own part in bringing our purpose to life." In this moment, Chip demonstrated how he was committed to our company's purpose and had contributed in a huge way to our overall success. His engagement in our purpose renewed our passion for the work we do. Show the folks who are doing the same at your organization that you value them. When they hit a big target, make sure they know what it means to you, the company, and to achieving your purpose.

CREATE NEW INITIATIVES

If your purpose makes big bold statements, you should be willing to back those statements up with action. You can't ask your employees to put purpose first if you don't create intentional space for that to happen. Let's say, for example, that your purpose is about innovation. Your people need to see that you are as committed to making big breakthroughs as your purpose says you are. They also need to know that you've put initiatives in place to make that innovative work possible. By

> If your purpose makes big bold statements, you should be willing to back those statements up with action. You can't ask your employees to put purpose first if you don't create intentional space for that to happen.

71

creating new initiatives, you will both equip your people to take on your purpose and will demonstrate to them that you are committed to bringing this purpose to life.

At 3M, a company you might know for its adhesive products, the purpose is *to solve unsolved problems innovatively*. To that end, the company carves out 15 percent of an employee's time to pursue some new idea, explore a passion, or create a new technology they have been dreaming up. This time has led to their people making some of the wildest things that have gone on to become part of the 3M business. From advanced data-analysis processes to innovative tooth-cleaning solutions, 3M has found a way to activate its purpose—for its business and for its people. The people at 3M have found a purpose that has ignited an engaged culture for those who are constantly asking themselves, "How can I make this better?"

You don't need to create a whole new charge code, however, to create an initiative based on your purpose. Consider creating formalized development initiatives such as book clubs or TED Talks to get your people engaged in your purpose. Moments like these allow your people to rise above their day-to-day tasks and think at a higher level about their work and the impact it has. It doesn't need to be huge—it just needs to feel right for your culture and your purpose.

A purpose is more than a poster: it is your people in action doing work that matters to them and to the world. A clear and unique purpose helps your people understand just exactly what they are doing and how what they are doing makes a larger impact. It creates a common language and idealism that will connect your people in a greater mission. A purpose statement, however, only answers the question, "Why?" In the next chapter, we'll explore how your people can help you answer the question, "How?"

ACTIVATE IT!

DEFINE IT

Purpose is a clear and unique statement that illustrates the fundamental answer to your organization's *why*.

- Gather a team of leaders and employees who have a vested interest in the success of the company.

- Hold a purpose-discovery meeting to get the answer to the question, "*Why* does our company do what it does?"

- Using these answers, write a clear and unique purpose statement that your people can see themselves in.

- Create a "purpose team" to spread the message of your purpose and to collect stories about your company's purpose in action.

LIVE IT OUT

- Connect your people to your purpose by mapping job descriptions, objectives, and priorities to the purpose.

- Save and share stories of success to demonstrate your purpose in action.

- Celebrate the milestones that move your purpose forward so your people will know that their work is valued.

- Bring in customers (or live examples of your purpose being lived out) to share their stories with your employees.

- Create new initiatives so your people can feel equipped to live out your company's purpose.

MAKE IT YOURS

- Why does your organization do what it does?

    - Why?

    - Why?

    - Why?

    - Why?

- Does your organization's purpose feel authentic to the company and your employees?

- What makes your purpose unique and different from your competitors?

- Do your employees know your company's stated purpose?

- Would your employees say your purpose is lived out authentically?

- Do your people feel their purpose in their everyday work? If not, how can you help them see their contributions?

- Which roles have a more direct effect on your company's purpose?

- How can you share the experience of the above roles with the rest of your organization?

ACTIVATE IT! NOTES

STEP THREE: DEFINE YOUR VALUES AND ACTIVATE YOUR CULTURE

*The ancient and eternal values of human life ...
are all statements of true belonging.*

—John O'Donohue

I n the journey of your company, the purpose gives you the road map. It's the North Star in the dark night that gives you the direction and the energy to attain your ultimate goal. How you get there, however, is entirely dependent on you and the people you travel with. The passions and attributes you all bring to the table in pursuing your purpose will show you the way. It's these core values that you all live every day that will help you continue to push your culture of engagement into the future.

Core values are the beliefs and principles of an organization's people in their pursuit of their purpose. If the purpose is the *why*, then your values are the *how*. These values serve as guiding principles for your organization to know how you'll accomplish your overall mission, how to make tough decisions, and, ultimately, how to work together in lockstep. At the tactical level, they are the standard for determining cultural fit for new hires and promotions as well as the barometer for deciding when an employee should be let go. Just like the purpose needs to be unique to your company, the core values must be specific to your people. They create an environment in which people can feel immediately if they fit in, or if they should move on. Culture fit isn't about having a culture of people who look and think the same, but it does mean that everyone aligns to the purpose and values and lives them out in their unique way.

> Culture fit isn't about having a culture of people who look and think the same, but it does mean that everyone aligns to the purpose and values and lives them out in their unique way.

This is your next step in creating a culture of engagement in your organization. **Defining your core values and cultural attributes** gives you a framework for how your business should be run and how decisions should be made. Clearly defining these values provides parameters for employees to explore and innovate. When a company activates these values and lives them out, it provides freedom for employees to explore new ideas and initiatives without the fear that they're heading in the wrong direction. You've provided them boundaries already in the values, but, as always, this action starts with you. As a leader, if you want to see your folks living your organization's values, you have to **activate these values by incorporating them into feedback, including them in your staffing decisions, and instituting a peer-recognition structure based on your values**. By keeping your values in mind while you make organizational decisions, you demonstrate to your people that your organization is a place where they belong, and where they can feel safe bringing their best selves to work.

HOW DO YOU CREATE YOUR COMPANY'S VALUES?

Right now, think about your organization. Is there one employee who sticks out? Someone whom the company would not be the same without? Who is that person? Is it more than just one? Write those names down now. Here, I'll even give you a space to do it:

_____

_____

_____

_____

_____

_____

Great. That person is what I like to call a "cultural rock star." This rock star is the living embodiment of your company and its values. You might have multiple names on this list, or just one. That's just fine! Others in your organization might also have suggestions of folks they know who are cultural rock stars. Listen to them, and gather all these people together to discuss the cornerstones of your organization. This group should be made up of people from various levels in your organization, with a wide array of perspectives and ideas. These folks will be critical in helping you articulate your cultural attributes and your core values. Some participants in this team may also be part of your purpose team, which is fine; just make sure that it's not the exact same team so you avoid creating an echo chamber. With this team assembled, host a session with the aim to uncover some of these values. It should be at least three to four hours in a setting where everyone feels comfortable and secure enough to speak their mind. Oh, and there should be plenty of scratch paper and pencils for people to jot down notes.

The first thing we do in these kinds of sessions is follow an exercise we learned from a company called Zingerman's, which is, oddly enough, a deli. But the company specializes in vision-creation strategies and share them with others across the world. The one I've used is called the "vision of greatness" exercise, and it'll require your people to think big about what they do. Ask your team to imagine the organization on a specific day five years in the future, and, for ten to fifteen minutes, write about what the culture is like on that day. This is called a "hot pen" exercise—participants should keep writing like the pen is hot and they can't stop. The key is to write continuously without worrying about grammar, narrative, or logical flow. Once they've done that, have them read their visions out loud and ask the other participants to jot down themes and key words they hear on Post-it notes.

With the Post-it notes, create a visual "heat map," grouping words that are similar on a wall or some other surface. Themes should now begin to emerge. Try to simplify these words again to create a list of potential values. These values should each have a name and a little subtext on how that value relates to the larger company purpose. After you're done with that, take a break: you've come a long way already. Let the ideas that have come out of this exercise sit with your people for some time. As you return to the "real world," you'll all notice how these themes and values live out in day-to-day interactions. When you see that, you know you've got a good thing going.

Schedule a second session with these same folks. It shouldn't be so close to the first session that they're still creatively exhausted, but also not so far away that they've forgotten everything they've covered. Put version one of your values up on a white board or other big screen and include any other themes that still seem relevant. At this point, you should have as many as six to eight key themes. Any more and we find that people get confused or distracted. Spend some time reading each one out loud. Ask yourself and the participants: "What's resonating? What doesn't fit? What—if anything—is missing? Where is there overlap?" Your goal in this exercise is to get to the essence of your values. And don't be afraid to cut something. If it isn't making sense to you, or it is already covered by another value, cut it! Once you've narrowed the list down even further (ideally four to six items), begin creating bullets underneath each theme that are methods of measuring this value. Review these bullets with your management team to verify that they can assess if and how their employees are living out the values. It's important that you make these behaviors as concrete as possible so that your people can understand if they're living out the value.

At this point, the values should be unique and memorable, and they should speak to specific aspects of your organization. You should also gather stories from your organization that you feel embody those values. Start small break-out groups throughout your teams to share the values and the supporting themes that accompany them. Then ask the employees to think back to a time on their team when they saw the value being lived out. Document these stories, as they will be useful for your launch and to help the company immediately have examples of each value in the wild. Once you're done with session two, you should have a list of concrete values supported by actionable items and valuable cultural stories. The final step—tell your people.

As with any great milestone you achieve, there should be a celebration—a launch party to introduce your people to a new system of values. But that's only the first part. Just like your purpose, if you put your values up on a wall and don't incorporate them into your culture, they become meaningless. You should look for ways to activate your values in your day-to-day culture. These methods of activation can take several forms, but in order to create an engaged culture, you must weave these values into your daily cadence of business.

INTEGRATE VALUES INTO HIRING DECISIONS

One of the first ways to activate your values is by integrating them directly into the hiring process. Starting from the beginning is indeed a beautiful place to start. If you get hiring right, then you'll be surprised by how many of these tips become so much easier. When you're interviewing candidates, ask them questions that directly relate to your values. If one of your values is about courage, for example, then ask them, "When was the last time you stood up for something you believed in?" Allowing them to speak directly to your values will help you—and them—understand whether or not they are a fit for your organization.

One way to activate your values in your hiring decisions is to create a rubric for how you're evaluating your applicants that uses the values as guideposts. This will give your hiring team a shared language, provide objectivity, and help them as they conduct their interviews. As I'm sure you know, hiring is hard and sometimes very expensive. But turnover, as we've seen, is quite costly as well. It's critical that you get hiring right to avoid losing an employee because they weren't the right fit.

Lastly, don't feel like you're alone in making this decision. At this point, you should have a small army of cultural rock stars who know your organization inside and out (likely they are the same people you wrote down early in the chapter). Bring them into the hiring process. This does two things: one, it gives the candidate an example of what an ideal employee looks like at this organization; and two, it emphasizes to your current employees that they have as big of a stake in this organization as you do. The more you can bring your people into big decisions like this, the more ownership they'll feel over the organization. That sense of ownership also leads to a sense of pride and engagement in the work they do every day.

When you integrate your cultural rock stars into your hiring process and empower them to have a voice in the decision making, you are laying a foundation of building a team of people who think like owners. It's a novel concept, but if you want your team acting like owners, you have to treat them as such. I highly recommend having someone on your team who is in the role you are hiring for participate in the hiring process. Leaders and executives dramatically underestimate the weight and prestige they bring into the interview. This can put up a wall between them and an interviewee so that they only have high-level conversations, reducing the type of authentic information they can receive. By integrating your employees into the hiring process (and training them well), you will quickly realize that they can get to the more practical, in-the-weeds information to help you make informed hiring decisions.

INCORPORATE VALUES INTO FEEDBACK

If values are there to guide your team, then you need to use them in a way that will help your people understand how they're doing. Incorporating your values into feedback can bring your values to life and make them real for your people. Every time you reward an employee or have to make a tough decision about their employment, make sure that decision is tied back to one of these values. With activated values, you now have two questions to ask to assess performance: "What were the results? How did you achieve those results?" The second one is a values assessment, making it clear that it's not just about achieving results; it's also about doing things in a way that lives out the values. This is where those actionable items I mentioned before are so important. Employees should be able to look at the core values and understand exactly how they are performing against each one of them. In addition, the core values provide a shared vocabulary for leaders and employees. This ensures that when you are providing feedback, it's as clear and as actionable as possible (more on this in the next chapter).

At the HR level, core competencies should directly relate to the core values of an organization. And because each employee's role and activity are different, you should translate how their behavior relates directly to the value. Let's say one of your core values is innovation. That value is going to look a lot different to an engineer than it is to an accountant. But if you can articulate the way that these values are expressed in different positions throughout the organization, you can encourage authentic and honest conversations between managers and staff. You can even use the stories you gathered earlier as a way to illustrate the values for your people. The values help make the feedback about the behavior instead of the person, which can make it more actionable and not as subjective. In that transparency, your people will have a clear directive that will help them become engaged in their work.

> The values help make the feedback about the behavior instead of the person, which can make it more actionable and not as subjective.

When your people exemplify a particular value, they should, of course, be recognized. If that is a promotion, make sure that when you publicize it, everyone at the organization knows exactly what value or values that employee represents. Doing this further brings your values to life and begins to give other employees a tangible example for particular values. They know, for example, that the new manager was given that promotion because they had a growth mindset when they identified their own growth areas and have worked tirelessly to gain the skills they need to close that gap. Your people should be able to see how these values play out in their day-to-day work so they can understand what good work means. By highlighting how these values are a part of their day-to-day, you're not just saying them; you're doing them.

USE VALUES IN PEER-TO-PEER RECOGNITION

While it's important to use the values in manager-to-employee feedback, your values won't catch on until everyone at your organization is using them. Your people should feel encouraged to nominate their peers as their own cultural rock stars for the rest of the organization to look up to. One way to do this is to create an awards system based on your values that is open for peer nomination. This will encourage the sharing of the values among your people and will make them feel like they have ownership over these values. They can point to specific peers and name the values they're living out in their actions.

There are plenty of ways to do this. I've heard of some companies that have created a corporate calendar where each month represents a different value—January for excellence, February for resilience, and so on and so forth. They then choose someone who exemplifies the value each month and recognize them at all-team meetings. Even quarterly recognition of individuals who live out your values can show your people your values in action. And then, at the end of the year, consider one "legend" or overall winner whom everyone could be jockeying for. I don't want to say that you're gamifying your values here, but a little friendly competition could help spur your people on to great things.

Other companies have used something called a "brag book" where employees can dedicate big things that other employees have done that they feel have lived up to the company's values. They use the book to publicly praise their teammates on a job well done. At the end of the year, they have a big ceremony where they read out everyone's accomplishments and then pick one person to dedicate that year's brag book to. Sounds a bit like a burn book from the movie *Mean Girls*, but much nicer. Any way you can get your people to feel like they own their values is a good thing in my book—pun very much intended.

A result of these peer nominations is that they give you a stockpile of stories on values to use in onboarding sessions, trainings, and other administrative tasks. One way you can make this easier on your folks is to create a "cultural playbook" that stores all the stories on values, any recognitions based on values, and any artifacts of culture. Yeah, I know that sounds like something from an Indiana Jones movie, but these artifacts are things that get the message out about your culture. Paper collateral, digital content, and videos are all examples of artifacts of culture, and they can be used to further make your values real. I've even heard of companies that give out stones with their values etched into them to high-performing employees. At Emplify, we use customized LEGOs with value logos printed on them to symbolize that our people are helping us build something great together.

PERQ—BRINGING VALUES TO THE GAME

Andy Medley, the CEO of PERQ, an Indianapolis-based marketing and web-development company, founded his company in the spirit of one phrase: "Game on!" At PERQ, the office is the playing field, and his people bring their whole selves to the game because they're 100 percent in on their core values. When they first created these values, Andy and his team analyzed the actions of the top players at his company to see what they brought to the playing field. What he found was that his people approached business as a game, and to PERQ, their values were the rules for how they played every day. In the spirit of this approach, they transformed their offices to reflect the power of these rules, creating massive murals that embodied the essence of each value. Immersing themselves in these values reminds all employees of what they're working for and how they can bring their best selves to the game.

And, of course, when you play a game, you've got to want to win. In an effort to recognize their strongest contributors and celebrate their day-to-day wins, the company created a live PERQ board game that now hangs on one of the walls. Employees can move their tokens ahead when a peer calls them out for an achievement inspired by one of PERQ's core values or when there is a massive customer win to be celebrated. This board game brings a sense of fun and play that is vital for PERQ's people to accomplish their success. PERQ is a great example of a company activating its values and living them in a way that is completely authentic.

NETFLIX—VALUES ON DEMAND

Netflix is another great example of a company activating its culture in a way that engages its people and energizes its business. Netflix's culture is based on deep-rooted values that have energized a workforce to dominate the entertainment industry. In 2009, the company's chief talent officer at the time, Patty McCord, created a presentation called "Netflix Culture." In it, she bluntly laid out a set of values that all the employees could see themselves in. Seriously, if you get a chance, you should read this document. The values are expertly written and clearly demonstrate to prospective and current employees what is part of Netflix's culture and what is not. Honesty and authenticity are held to a high standard, which is expressed through the company's approach to feedback and how it handles gossip. The company does not tolerate adequacy, per this document, stating that Netflix is not a family but a dream team. In the company's words: "A family is about unconditional love, despite, say, your siblings' bad behavior. A dream team is about pushing yourself to be the best teammate you can be, caring intensely about your teammates, and knowing that you may not be on the team forever."[18]

If teammates don't align to the values, Netflix is quick to part ways with them, but they won't just leave them empty handed. When and if this happens, they offer the employee a substantial severance package so they can find the organization that's right for them. This manifesto also helps Netflix with finding the right talent. It so perfectly lays out what it means to be a Netflix employee that

---

18   "Netflix Culture," https://jobs.netflix.com/culture.

potential recruits can read it and see whether or not they'd be good fits for the company. The best values allow potential employees to opt out on their own. These clear definitions and honest value statements show how a company's culture can create an engaged and empowered workforce. It's clear that the leadership at Netflix put in the time to think about what makes and keeps a culture engaged. And act on it.

*   *   *

Values, together with purpose, create a common vernacular that gives people a vision of the future with the guardrails to play in. When they are truly activated, they help employees and executives alike see where they are going and how they're going to get there. They are a North Star that guides the journey of your organization and its people. Now that you've illuminated that for them at the macro level, it's time to ask them what they think their own personal *why* is, and how that can fit into the business. It's in that overlap that you cultivate trust and a bond that will keep your employees working as hard as they can for your organization's goals.

ACTIVATE IT!

DEFINE IT

Core Values are the beliefs and principles of an organization's people in the pursuit of their purpose.

- Create a peer-nominated team of cultural rock stars.

- Host a session that begins with Zingerman's "vision of greatness" exercise.

- Create a visual heat map of Post-its to see what themes are emerging.

- Consolidate to four to six themes to home in on your values.

- Create a list of examples to help define value and determine if it is being lived out.

- Launch your values with a celebration that includes sharing stories of cultural rock stars living them out.

LIVE IT OUT

- Add a "How" section to your performance reviews to assess if employees are exemplifying core values while they're completing their day-to-day tasks.

- Create a peer-nominated award system tied to your values.

- Integrate your values into staffing by:

  - creating interview questions that assess whether the applicant shares the same values;

  - bringing cultural rock stars into the interview process and weaving the values into job descriptions for open roles.

MAKE IT YOURS

- Who are the employees that embody what you want your culture to look like?

- What are the stories that best illustrate your values?

- How can you incorporate your values into your feedback with direct reports?

- How can you optimize your hiring process to better screen for the value fit of candidates?

- In what ways can you reinforce your values throughout your organization?

ACTIVATE IT! NOTES

_____

_____

_____

_____

_____

_____

_____

_____

_____

_____

_____

_____

_____

_____

_____

_____

_____

_____

_____

_____

CHAPTER EIGHT

STEP FOUR: SET GOALS WITH YOUR TEAM

Working hard for something we do not care about is called stress. Working hard for something we love is called passion.

—Simon Sinek, *Start with Why: How Great Leaders Inspire Everyone to Take Action*

A couple of years ago, I was giving a talk on motivating and engaging workforces at a conference for business leaders that was hosted at the event center of a hotel. That evening, after I had finished speaking, I went to the hotel bar to grab a bite to eat. There was a young man sitting at the bar with me who looked like he had clearly lost several nights of sleep. He looked up from his drink, locked eyes, and came over to join me. Frazzled, he admitted that he had attended my session and just wanted to discuss some follow-up questions. He had recently been promoted to manager at his company but, as soon as he took on the new position, felt like all the motivation had been drained out of his team. This was his first time as a manager, and he really wanted to prove that he could do a good job for his company. The reality of the situation, however, was that his people were disengaged, causing him an immense amount of stress.

From his first day at the company, this young man had always known he wanted to be on the management track. He worked his way through the organization as a hard worker and a great individual contributor, ultimately achieving his goal to become a manager. As soon as he was promoted, he began to implement the techniques that had worked for him. As he had accomplished his goals, he thought he could help his people by taking them on the same journey he had taken. Unfortunately, his staff resisted this move and distanced themselves from their ex-colleague. He was at his wit's end and had no idea what to do next. At this point, I put down my knife and fork and asked him, "Do you think you're managing your people the way *you* want to be managed or the way *they* want to be managed?"

One of the biggest mistakes managers make is to assume what motivates them also motivates their employees. These managers think that their *why* is the same as their employees' *why*. I briefly mentioned the concept of a **personal *why*** in the first part of this book, but I'd like to further explore it here. To start, a personal why is a deep passion in people's lives that gives them direction and meaning, and motivates them to take action; it's the answer to the age-old question, "Why were you put on this earth?" The concept of *why* as a motivating factor for people was first introduced to me in Simon Sinek's book *Start with Why*. In his book, Sinek puts forward that we all have our own personal reasons for why we do what we do. Much like an organization has a purpose, individuals too must have a reason behind the decisions they make. Simon posits that for leaders to motivate their staff, they need to know what drives them to come into work every day—they need to know their people's *why*. In my years as a manager, I've found that the best way to help folks articulate their personal *why* is by helping them set goals.

Just as a purpose can help an organization set business priorities, a personal *why* is fundamental in helping individuals create their own goals. These goals can be personal or professional, but they are always motivated by a person's needs, desires, and passions. As a leader, you should be able to name the specific motivating factors for each of your employees and how you can help them achieve their own goals—both at work and at home. When you understand the goals and motivations of your people, you can help them unlock their own potential and encourage them to work toward what they've set out to do.

Practically, this helps your people bring their best selves to work every day. By creating manageable goals, they know that their work is connected to some bigger achievement and that leadership will have their back in reaching those goals. While for some folks, their *why* might be a promotion or a different position within a company, others might have different goals that exist outside the walls of your organization (likely they'll have both). It's your job as a leader to help connect the dots between what your employees are doing now, what they will do in the future, and how their actions will help them toward their *why*. In connecting these dots, you will motivate your people to do good work in a way that feels authentic to their own personal *why*. Remember, it's likely that these motivations are not related to compensation or benefits anymore. These personal *whys* are the deep-rooted values of your people, and understanding them is critical to how you can lead them in their work. In order to make this real for you and your people, **first identify their *why* and their goals**. Next, **help them map out a plan to achieve those goals**. Finally, as you work with them, **hold them accountable to that plan**. In following these three steps, you'll come to better understand what motivates your people and how you can work with them to make those goals a reality.

IDENTIFY THEIR *WHY* AND THEIR GOALS

When you work with your people to identify their *why* and set their goals, you as a leader need to act as a vision caster for them—showing them a future that could be. Take some time to meet with them individually about their goals, either individually or in a group setting. There are benefits to both, but what's most important is that you create an environment where the employees feel safe sharing their innermost thoughts. When you establish this atmosphere of psychological safety, you can talk openly and honestly with your people about their goals and how you can help get them there.

One of my previous direct reports, Chris, said that his goal for the year was to take his kids to Disney World. An admirable goal, for sure, and one I was happy to help him with, but I was curious: Why Disney World? Why was that what he wanted to spend his time working toward? Upon further reflection, Chris admitted he wanted to spend more time with his kids and create moments that would result in lasting memories for his family. He knew in order to do this, he'd have to up his sales numbers to increase his commission. In this way, he was directly linking the work he was doing every day to a more meaningful and measurable goal: to save up enough discretionary income to take his family to Disney World. His goal now had a tangible objective, something he could see growth in. Getting to the root of a goal will help you and your employees

> Getting to the root of a goal will help you and your employees best understand what they'll need to do to achieve it.

best understand what they'll need to do to achieve it.

If you've established psychological safety throughout your teams, you can have annual goal-setting meetings where everyone—leaders included—dream up their goals and plans for the year. Psychological safety was one of the seventeen drivers that contribute to engagement defined in chapter four, but to review, it's a feeling of security established by a leader's authentic behavior that allows employees to share their perspective without fear of retribution. This security is essential in creating a culture in your workforce where feedback isn't feared; it's encouraged. When you unlock psychological safety in your teams, you create the potential for continual improvement, both in your processes and in your people (more on this in the next chapter). This safety is critical in helping you and your people get to the bottom of what actions need to be taken in pursuit of their goals.

But, back to how you set these goals. First, you need a moment where you all can step away from your day-to-day operations and get a bigger perspective on things. On my teams, we've done these meetings the second week of January every year. We've found this works well because, for us, January is the start of a new calendar and fiscal year, and folks are often thinking about their future. Setting aside this time for your people gives them the freedom to make big and lofty goals and sets a foundation for managers and staff as they move forward into the new year. It also gives them a moment to reconnect to their purpose, the company's purpose, and the values that support the same. As a leader, you can work with your people to break these goals down into measurable steps and strategies that will work within your business. Also, make sure you help connect the dots between the objectives of their roles and how those objectives connect to their *why*. This will help your people see the results of their work clearly, and, in turn, create more engagement in the work they do day to day. By taking the time to set these goals, your people will gain direction in their work, and you will gain insight into how you can manage them most effectively.

While there are many ways to host these kinds of goal-setting sessions, I'm going to let you in on the process I've found works the best for me. The first thing we do is have each person write down what their professional and personal goals are for this year. A **professional goal** can be a position that an employee wants to take on, a skill they'd like to learn, or a new client they'd like to work with—something that deals with their day-to-day work. **Personal goals** are things they'd like to achieve outside the workplace: "I'd like to spend more time with my kids," "I'd like to become more active," or "I want to start a specific hobby" are all examples of personal goals.

After they've written down these goals, we ask them to consider what about their life makes these goals important right now. Why is now the right time to take on that promotion or get fit? This further roots the goal in their personal *why* and allows you to further understand the timeline for how you can help them realize these goals. Some balance or integration of their goals and their *why* will help to identify what their specific motivations are at work. Also, look for where their individual goals can connect to the company's purpose and core values. For instance, if a personal goal is to gain a specific skill set and a core value is growth mindset, then you can mention how taking on their individual goal is a great example of living out an established value. This will help you and your employees understand their motivations and will show you how to lead them from a place of empathy—like a human would.

HELP THEM MAP OUT A PLAN TO ACHIEVE THEIR GOALS

Once they've identified their goals and the reasons behind them, it's time to get them thinking about how they can get there. First off, you should do the homework of understanding how you can connect their personal goals and professional goals with their current job. Let's take Chris for example. He wanted to take his family to Disney World. In order to do that, I knew he'd need to increase his sales so that he could take the time off he needed, and so he could save up enough to pay for it. Now, I know I've said over and over that compensation and benefits do not create engagement, but in Chris's situation, money was something he needed to achieve a deeper goal: to spend more time with his family. And if he upped his sales numbers, he'd get more commission that he could then bank for that trip. He had his goal set, and together we mapped out what he needed to do to achieve his goal. When you know how these things can be linked, you can then work with your own folks to create a development plan.

First off, your people need to identify the blockers or hurdles that stand in their way of achieving their goals. When I work with my people, I ask them to write down anything that might be keeping them from their goals and any ways that they might already be working toward them. This gets the wheels turning about the small changes they need to make in their day to achieve that bigger goal. For some it might be waking up earlier to have more time to read, take a class, or go for a run. For others it might be improving their listening skills or asking better questions. There are no right or wrong answers here. The power in this process is having your people thoughtfully list out what things need to change in their life for them to accomplish their goals. If nothing needs to change—then they would have already achieved their goals!

HOLD THEM AND YOURSELF ACCOUNTABLE

Finally, encourage accountability about these goals among your people. When we do these goal-setting sessions with our staff, we give everyone the space to share what they've written down with their team—if they feel comfortable sharing, that is. This is where it's important that leaders are also in the room. When your people see that their leaders have created their own sets of goals—and, more importantly, named habits in their own lives that need to change—it establishes that psychological safety and gives the team permission to open up and be vulnerable. Sharing goals also makes your employees accountable to their whole team for their success.

Chris announced his goal of Disney World to the team during a goal-setting workshop so his team could keep an eye on how he was doing. One of the ways he said he would get there was by increasing his percentage of sales by a certain amount. Halfway through the year, it was becoming clear to him and the team that he wasn't hitting the target he had set for himself. We were all going over the team's numbers in a meeting one day, and, when we got to his performance numbers, a colleague of his, Kayla, ribbed him, asking, "Hey, how's that trip to Disney World coming?"

That next month, our intrepid Mouseketeer got motivated, turned around his performance, and nearly doubled his sales numbers. That nudging comment about his planned trip was the exact push he needed and helped to remind him of the goal he was working for. The group knew that this goal was something he was striving for, and they held him accountable to that. While a callout like this might not work for everyone, group accountability gives your employees a partner in their journey. They know that each person might have a different set of goals but that they're all working toward them together. And the most critical accountability partner is you—the leader.

That goal-setting session Chris attended was in 2017. As of the publication of this book in 2020, he has taken his kids to Disney every year since then. Chris is a shining example of what happens when you can directly link an employee's work to their personal *why*. We connected his sales performance to his personal desire to spend more time with his kids. When he found that connection, he worked hard and put in extra discretionary effort to make that goal a reality. As a result, his sales numbers had never been better. It's a pretty cool story, if you ask me. If that doesn't sound like an employee engaging their full potential at work, well then, I don't know what does!

Once you have aligned with your team on their goals at the start of the year, it's important that you have regular cadences to help track toward their goals and their performance. We'll talk more about this in the next chapter, but much of the work of bringing these goals to life comes in the form of weekly one-on-ones and quarterly conversations. A good place to start is to have regular touch-base meetings with each member of your staff in a cadence that fits the needs of you and your team. In these meetings, you should be discussing what progress your people are making in their goals and brainstorming ways you can help them in their pursuit. What's important is that you use these times to envision with your employees what their future could look like, and how you can open up opportunities to get them where they want to be. As a leader, one of the best things you can do is to help an employee find their personal *why*, and goal setting in this way is a tangible way to do that.

Your team is made up of many individuals with their own unique wants, needs, passions, and desires. Together, these things make up each of their unique personalities, with their own sets of motivators. In order to lead like a human, you should know that your people are humans as well. They want to be unlocked to do the best work they can, and it's your job to help show them the way. They'll need your guidance and perspective along on the journey, and, in supporting them through this, you can unlock the potential of your team.

> In order to lead like a human, you should know that your people are humans as well. They want to be unlocked to do the best work they can, and it's your job to help show them the way.

ACTIVATE IT!

DEFINE IT

A **personal *why*** is a deep-seated, fundamental purpose that motivates a person to take action, as outlined by Simon Sinek in *Start with Why*.

Goals are achievable objectives driven by a person's *why* and realized through a structured action plan.

Psychological safety, one of the seventeen drivers that contribute to engagement, is a feeling of security established by a leader's authentic behavior that allows employees to share their perspective without fear of retribution.

- Set aside time to work with your people to set their goals. Ideally, do this in a group setting. If not, one-on-one sessions are also effective.

- Ask your team to think about and write down their personal and professional goals.

- Identify any habits they need to change to achieve their goals.

- Work with them to create a plan to achieve those goals, and check in periodically on their progress.

LIVE IT OUT

- Do your homework to understand how you can link their professional and personal goals to their role.

- Meet with them regularly to see how they're doing on their documented plan, and hold them accountable.

- With established psychological safety, encourage everyone to share their goals with their colleagues—that includes you.

MAKE IT YOURS

- What goals have you personally set for this year—both professional and personal?

- What blockers or challenges are keeping you from attaining these goals?

- Do you have a documented plan listing your goals and the steps necessary to achieve them?

- Do you have someone to help hold you accountable?

- What are the goals of each of your employees, and how are you helping them achieve them?

- Is there a common thread among all your people's goals that you can use to motivate them together or have groups lean on each other?

ACTIVATE IT! NOTES

_____

_____

_____

_____

_____

_____

_____

_____

_____

_____

_____

_____

_____

_____

_____

_____

_____

_____

_____

CHAPTER NINE

STEP FIVE: CREATE A CULTURE OF CONTINUAL IMPROVEMENT

Improvement starts with I.

–Arnold Glasow

Sometimes it's easy to forget the hard work people have put into the things we now take for granted. Take electric lighting, for example. In 1879, Thomas Edison created the first incandescent light bulb in his laboratory in Menlo Park, New Jersey. For most of us, that's the end of the story. Edison invented the light bulb. Case closed. But to think that he made this world-shattering innovation completely alone in a single night is just laughable. As a matter of fact, that first light bulb only burned for a few short hours and then fizzled out. It took months of trial and error with his lab team to land on the specific bulb shape, electrical wiring, and filament structure to bring his innovation to life. In fact, Edison and his team tested over six thousand different materials to be used in the filament—the part that glows to create light—before they landed on the right material: carbonized cotton. When Edison and his team found that it had been glowing for fifteen hours, they celebrated. They'd invented something that would change the world.

We all know the famous Edison quote about invention being mostly composed of perspiration, but there's another quote of his that I think better demonstrates his grit and drive: "Nearly every man who develops an idea works it up to the point where it looks impossible, and then he gets discouraged. That's not the place to become discouraged."[19] At Menlo Park, Edison worked with his team to continually push themselves to create the next invention, the next big thing that would make life easier for everyone. Over four hundred patents came out of that laboratory, some of which inspired huge disruptions in multiple industries—motion pictures, the stock ticker, and phonographs, to name a few. Edison was never satisfied with solving just one impossible problem and insisted that the scientists he led felt the same. While he gave some guidance at their workbenches, Edison encouraged his people to find their own solutions in their day-to-day experiments.[20] In their consistent drive to do more, Edison and his engaged team created a culture of continual improvement in their laboratory.

While we all aren't on a mission to create the next light bulb, you should have your own higher company purpose that can guide you. We can learn from Edison and his cohort at Menlo Park and how they activated a culture of continual improvement to achieve their purpose. Continual improvement is the consistent pursuit of self-development in an organization's workforce that drives radical growth in its business. In the last chapter, we went over how setting goals can help motivate and engage your teams. But what happens when you achieve that goal? In a culture of continual improvement,

---

19   "Edison's Lightbulb," The Franklin Institute Archives, https://www.fi.edu/history-resources/edisons-lightbulb.

20   Paul B. Israel, "The Year of Innovation: The Invention Factory," Thomas A. Edison Papers, October 2016, http://edison.rutgers.edu/inventionfactory.htm#7.

you look ahead to the next one. As people set goal after goal, they are putting their discretionary effort toward improving themselves. This constant forward motion in their careers, in turn, leads to engagement in their work. Multiply this by the amount of people you lead, and you've got an engaged workforce continually working on improving themselves and your business. The first step toward creating this culture of continual improvement actually starts with you and your own commitment to growth. Once you've demonstrated that to your people, you can continue to activate this culture by putting yourself in their shoes and creating a consistent cadence of feedback in their development plan.

IT STARTS WITH YOU

In reading this book, you have taken your first step in realizing your own personal growth. So congratulations! You've also taken the first step toward creating a culture of continual improvement in your organization. Taking the time to better understand how you can grow yourself requires an incredible amount of vulnerability. When your people know you are committed to your own improvement, they know that they can be honest with you about their own paths toward growth. This is one reason it is so important for leaders to attend those goal-setting sessions we discussed in the previous chapter. As a leader, being open about your own development plan fosters a culture of continual improvement that begins at the top and works its way down throughout the entire organization.

In one of our goal-setting sessions at Emplify, we once had a manager stand up and say that he was making it a goal to listen more in meetings. He had gotten some feedback that he had a tendency to talk over folks in meetings and ignore their proposals in favor of his own. By openly sharing this goal with his team, he showed them that he was committed to taking their feedback and growing himself. This manager unlocked psychological safety and trust in his team, which gave them the permission to give him feedback. Safety is the key to creating a culture where innovation can thrive, where ideas are shared openly and freely, and where broken processes are flagged and fixed. That openness alone made communication with him so much easier and allowed his people to feel safe bringing their ideas to the table. By simply stating an area for personal improvement, a leader can demonstrate that they're also pursuing growth in their own way—just like their employees.

> Safety is the key to creating a culture where innovation can thrive, where ideas are shared openly and freely, and where broken processes are flagged and fixed.

In naming your own growth area, you do three things: you make it a real commitment to yourself and your team, you subconsciously give your people permission to work on themselves, and you create a healthy atmosphere in your team where feedback is encouraged. These three things have the potential to forge a trusted and authentic relationship with your people. There is a humility that comes from self-improvement that says "I'm also trying to get better. I haven't arrived. I need to improve." In order to lead like a human, you must display this humility. Failure is human and an essential part of this growth. If you falter on your own journey, don't try to cover it up. Show your folks your missteps so that they can see you're human too. Failure isn't only acceptable in a culture of continual improvement; it's encouraged. Failure sets you up for success.

Another way you can demonstrate that you're committed to your own growth is to find a mentor. I first learned this when Emplify experienced a period of substantial change that demanded I go from managing five folks to over twenty. Obviously, I was learning to lead on a completely new scale—it was time for me to be stretched again, and I knew I needed an outside perspective. That's how I was connected to Derek Grant, who was a VP at SalesLoft. He agreed to provide that perspec-

> Failure isn't only acceptable in a culture of continual improvement; it's encouraged. Failure sets you up for success.

tive, and we set up a day where I shadowed him while he took meetings, met with staff, and worked with his clients. He let me sit in on each of his appointments (even his one-on-ones) as if I were just a member of his own team. That's right, I took an entire day to travel to SalesLoft headquarters and invest in my own growth. At the end of our day together, he set aside a couple of hours where he could answer any questions that came up and reflect on the day. I jotted down his responses and took what I'd learned back to my team. In an introductory meeting to my new and much larger team, I went over with them exactly what I'd learned from Derek and how I'd be implementing it into my current goal plan. I wanted them to know that I was preparing myself for this new task and that they should feel safe with me at the helm. While I might have never said it out loud, I was demonstrating to my people that I was pushing myself to grow and that I encouraged and expected the same behavior from them.

When you're open about your own development, you can be direct and candid with the feedback you give your people because you are both striving for improvement. You've created a commonality between you and your people. And your employees will likely embrace the feedback, knowing you're on your own journey toward your own goals. This kind of feedback is a key driver in creating engaged cultures. Employees today are hungry for authenticity and self-development. When you display a willingness to receive feedback, it makes your people want the same kind of feedback. It's when their desire for feedback meets your clarity of direction that magic happens. They improve as you grow. It's a cycle that keeps building as your company pursues its purpose.

> When you display a willingness to receive feedback, it makes your people want the same kind of feedback. It's when their desire for feedback meets your clarity of direction that magic happens.

PUT YOURSELF IN THEIR SHOES

Another way to cultivate this trusted relationship between you and your people is to put yourself in their shoes. Occasionally, you should do the jobs that you task your people with in order to see the world through their eyes. From participating on the factory floor to recording yourself doing sales calls, these actions will grow trust between management and staff in almost any industry. That trust drives engagement in your people and also gives you a much-needed perspective shift. Once a month, open yourself up to taking on your people's jobs, and you'll see they're tougher than you might expect, which will give you insights into broken systems or opportunities for efficiency. I've done this at Emplify before, and, let me tell you, it's been illuminating.

One time, I was sitting in the chair of a sales rep, trying to make some calls that could result in a lead. I had my script in front of me and my headset on, and I was ready to schedule some meetings. I picked up the phone, made a call, and, before I could even get the first words of my intro out, the line went dead. I had been rejected in the coldest way possible: I was hung up on. Instead of trying to hide it, however, I sent it as a Slack message to some of my staff: "Help me out here," I said. "What could I have done differently?"

Doing your employees' jobs not only shows your humility (especially when you ask for feedback) but also builds empathy for you as a leader. They can see you aren't just managing detached from what they do every day—you're wrestling with the same things they're struggling with. This demonstrates a level of vulnerability in you, and it shows that you understand their perspective because you've taken the time to see the world from their eyes. This furthers an open and authentic relationship between you and your people where everyone can be open about the pain points in your processes and what can be done about them.

Say, for instance, a manager at a factory comes down and works on the line for a shift. During this shift, this manager will experience the kinks or problems in the system firsthand, and any aspects of the job that are unnecessarily difficult will come into focus. At that point, the manager can go to the team and ask honestly if this is something that has been affecting their performance. Now that both parties are aware of the problem, they can work together to solve it, eliminating the problem altogether. Taking this action further helps solidify that relationship of trust between you and your staff. This solid relationship encourages engagement in your team and helps everyone create a work environment where they can thrive.

CONSISTENT AND STEADY RHYTHMS FOR FEEDBACK

In order to foster a culture of continual improvement, you have to have a workforce dedicated to their own personal and professional development. While I mentioned in the last chapter that the most concrete way of doing this is to set goals, your people also need a plan of action to achieve those goals. And, as their leader, you should know your people's goals inside and out. You should have a scheduled weekly one-on-one with each member of your team to discuss how they're actualizing these plans and how you can help them along the way. A consistent and steady rhythm of feedback will help your people see how they're progressing in their development and is a key driver to creating an engaged workforce.

These one-on-ones aren't only for talking about goals or banging out a task list together. They're meant to create a strong foundation for your relationships with your people. To that end, these weekly meetings should have a balance of tasks, goals, rapport, and feedback. It's essential that you use this time to continue building a solid relationship with your employees, where you feel you can give constructive feedback that will be received. This simple change in relationship is often what most unlocks the potential in your employees. They know they want to grow, but to get better they need feedback from having a trusting relationship with a manager whom they feel they can trust. Think of these meetings as road markers on your employees' journey where you can help encourage them along in a way that's authentic and true to everyone.

While you're holding the space for these one-on-ones, consider that these are the moments where you bring to fruition for an individual everything that we've discussed in the past couple of chapters. You should be helping tie their role to their purpose so they can see where they fit into the organization. You should be coaching them to your company's values so that they can adjust their behavior accordingly. Give them the feedback on their goals that they need and discuss the roadblocks that keep them from achieving them. And most importantly, take some time to learn who they are and how they tick. Establish your own rapport that's individual for each of your people. Doing this sounds like a lot, but when you've scheduled them with enough time to reflect on what you'll talk about in these meetings, it should be manageable. These are meetings for your employees, so guide them but ensure you're giving them the time for what they need.

While I have my own way of holding these meetings, you should focus on creating a style that works for you. My method for conducting these one-on-ones has largely been informed by the *Manager Tools Podcast*. (If you haven't subscribed, I highly encourage you to go check it out now.) Whatever way you decide to hold them, having regular touch-bases with your people is vital in creating a culture where everyone is growing.

First thing, **I always let the employee start the meeting**. Maybe they've come in with an entire agenda that they want to cover with bullet points, questions, and key objectives. That's great! Maybe they just want to talk to you about the latest show they watched for ten minutes. That's great too! This is their time, and you should set up your meetings to reflect that. If they aren't quite sure where to start, I ask them to pick a color—red, yellow, or green—to reflect on how they're showing up today. This is another tactic I gleaned from Reboot, the coaching company I mentioned before. Red means there's something majorly wrong. They have a pressing issue or fire and aren't showing up present for the meeting. Yellow means they are doing okay. Not feeling their best, but also not their worst. Usually something is off here, but not majorly wrong—a great opportunity as their manager to help uncover what it is! Green means they feel great and positive and are showing up in a good place.

Again, these are only examples of how you interpret these colors: you're simply asking this open-ended question to see how they're showing up. Just like we talked about in chapter five, naming your feelings help you address them. As a leader, guiding your employees through some self-reflection helps them understand how they're showing up and what they can do to feel more balanced and productive. This is especially important if you are just starting out with an employee. If this is one of those initial meetings, consider some of the following questions for openers as well:

- What are you most excited about in this season at work?

- Where do you think you have the most opportunity to grow, and how can I help you with that?

- If you were in my shoes, what would be your top priority?

- What concerns about having a new manager do you have that might be good for us to talk through?

- You know yourself well—tell me about the best relationship you've had with a manager, and what made that person effective.

These are all great starting places as you take on a new member of your team. Having these consistent meetings demonstrates to your people that you are as interested in their growth as they are. As your relationship grows through these meetings, you should begin to see a change in their behavior. They will become more engaged in accomplishing daily tasks because they'll see how they're linked to their overall goals. They'll see how small daily steps can make a big achievement over time.

KNOW THEIR JOURNEY LIKE YOUR OWN

As you continue in these weekly one-on-ones, remember to focus on the progress they are making and not the end goal. You want them to feel that you know their journey as well as your own. Pursuing goals is a marathon, not a sprint, and they need endurance to get them where they want to be. Ask them how what they are doing today is affecting the shared goals you've outlined together. Do they feel closer to their goal or farther away? You want to use your time together to show them how what they are doing now will affect where they are heading in the future.

In addition, you should always have one area of improvement that you want to bring up in your meetings. As you witness your people grow, these areas will become clearer to you, and hopefully to them. Remind them how the area of improvement you're bringing up will help them actualize their *why*. It's in these meetings where you can show them how the steps they're taking today—no matter how small—are moving them forward. Also, frame the feedback you give them within your organization's core values so they can see how their improvement will benefit the overall organization. Demonstrating progress shows your people how what they do matters—both to them and to the business.

Finally, schedule a quarterly meeting with your people as well to reflect on the larger scope of their journey. Quarterly conversations are a chance to go above the day-to-day and talk bigger about the future—performance, growth, and how their role is helping them live out their personal motivation. Because this meeting is meant to explore a bigger perspective, I recommend having this off-site (if you are able): somewhere you both feel comfortable and that gives you each a fresh perspective. While most companies have a structured yearly performance-review process for HR departments to address compensation, this shouldn't be the only time your team gets feedback from you. Again, these quarterly and weekly meetings are moments for you to help your people do their best work, achieve their higher goals, and grow into the people they were always meant to be.

In the lead-up to a quarterly meeting with your employee, assign them homework to review their accomplishments and growth areas from the last quarter and to come in with one named area of improvement for the next quarter. Take the time to review their work for yourself and come up with your own area of growth for them. If other managers are involved, ask them to review that employee's work and get their opinion on how this individual is doing. In the meeting, go over what you both have gleaned from looking back on the last quarter and what each of your areas of improvement are. Together, see where your two areas align and how the feedback can be tied to one of your organization's core values. Once you've checked how these areas align, agree upon an official growth area for this individual and spend the rest of the meeting discussing how you as a manager can best help in this journey. These quarterly check-ins help you evaluate the bigger picture of an employee's journey so that you can restrategize for the months ahead.

Now, you might be at an organization that has its own evaluation process that works. That's fantastic, and obviously, you should continue to use it. I would consider how you can incorporate these weekly touch-bases and quarterly conversations into the cadence of these evaluations. Could you align one of your quarterly meetings with the annual performance review? Are there designated times in the week where a touch-base would work best for you and your people? By going above and beyond what is expected of you as a manager, you are continuing to demonstrate that you're dedicated to your people's success. They'll thank you for it with their hard work.

When everyone in an organization embraces a culture of continual improvement, you give your people the sense that they're as responsible for the success of the organization as the top leaders in the company are. This creates a team where second best is just never good enough. In pursuing their own personal best, your people will unlock their collective power and create innovations you've never dreamed of—just like Thomas Edison and his Menlo Park cohort. In a culture of continual improvement, problems that were thought to be unsolvable are suddenly solved. Innovation begins to skyrocket because your people are putting their heads and hearts into their work. Making business decisions will become easier because you'll be guided by a strong workforce full of ideas and passion. That being said, you might not always have the answer, and that's okay. Humans aren't perfect, and failure is part of the journey toward growth.

ACTIVATE IT!

DEFINE IT

Continual improvement is the consistent pursuit of self-development in an organization's workforce that drives radical growth in its business.

- Be open and honest about your own development plan and the steps you are taking toward your growth.

- Meet with your people weekly to discuss their goals and development.

- Have a quarterly meeting with your people that explores the big picture of their goals and performance.

- Mutually name an opportunity for growth for the employee for the quarter.

LIVE IT OUT

- Develop a regular cadence where you can do your people's jobs so you can better understand their perspective and open up opportunities for improvement.

- In your one-on-ones, always let your people start the meeting so they can learn to guide their own growth.

- Develop a more authentic connection with your direct reports by learning their goals and plans.

- Identify areas of growth to help develop your people during their one-on-ones.

MAKE IT YOURS

- What is your own growth plan, and what objectives are you trying to accomplish?

- How are you letting your people in on your journey?

- What is your process for feedback, and does it allow for two-way communication?

- How can you create intentional time for getting closer to your employees' work?

- How are you taking time to help your people envision their goals in a way that will feel actionable?

ACTIVATE IT! NOTES

STEP SIX: USE DATA

I never guess. It is a capital mistake to theorize before one has data.

—Sir Arthur Conan Doyle

I n my time working with leaders from various industries, I've found that their biggest fear is the unknown. Indeed, the unknown is scary to all of us. If we don't fully comprehend the size or scope of a situation, we have a hard time making decisions. This anxiety can have huge negative impacts on how business leaders are heading their organizations, especially when it comes to their people's level of engagement. When leaders lack a clear vision into the state of their workforce, they could either be making decisions that promote broken processes or completely ignoring things that are already destroying their business. To show you what I mean, let me tell you about a client we worked with at Emplify who discovered that the cause of their biggest problem was where they least expected to find it.

This client was a small construction company based in the Midwest that coordinated building projects across the city where it operated. At this company, there was a certain site supervisor who had worked there for over fifteen years. The CEO pointed this guy out to me as one of their best—a trusted resource who always knew how to identify key problems at his site and communicate them back to leadership. Unfortunately, his projects always seemed to fall apart despite his allegedly strong performance. They brought us in to help them figure out why this kept happening despite their best attempts to curtail the crumbling projects. In order to get to the bottom of the issue, we ran our own survey and analysis to uncover clues from their employees.

Turns out that the data we gathered from this process painted a less-than-appealing picture of their top-performing site supervisor. The data pointed back to him as the epicenter for the mismanagement problems. When it came to his projects falling apart, all the failures and missteps were due to his poor management skills, which he'd been able to cover up by maintaining a good working relationship with upper management. When we showed the findings to the CEO, he was shocked at what was actually going on at his company. What happened here was a classic case of a middle manager who was very good at managing up, but terrible at handling his staff in the day-to-day. In these kinds of situations, where you have an employee who's basically a fixture at your company, it's easy to let personal relationships get in the way of sound business decisions. After the CEO took in the feedback from his people, he realized that he had been building strategy on intuition, as opposed to relying on clear and actionable data.

Twenty years ago, management was about making decisions from your gut, intuition, instinct, and watercooler talk. Leaders couldn't accurately predict what impact something would have on their business because they lacked baseline employee-engagement data. Instead, they relied on anecdotal evidence they'd gleaned from hallway conversations. For example, someone might say, "Hey, I heard George talking about how we could use more PTO at the firm." The next quarter, there'd be a 20 percent raise in PTO hours across the board.

At the time, the company lacked scientific visibility into the hearts and minds of its team. The company didn't have access to the data that would help to best understand the state of the workforce, because the methods and means of gathering this information hadn't been perfected yet. There was no metric that could show the true engagement of the company's people, only unhelpful comments about employee satisfaction based on a survey with a handful of ineffective questions, as we covered a couple of chapters back. Without this data, managers were in the dark about how to create the right environment for their people to do their best work.

Today, we live in a world full of data. From smart thermometers in our homes to sensors on the factory lines, we're able to track and measure things we never before thought possible. These advancements have even changed how sport coaches train and manage their players. Data, if used well, can have the power to revolutionize how leaders engage their people. They no longer need to rely on their intuition or instinct or even the loudest voice in the room when making decisions. Data gives these leaders a heat map to the problems within their organization so they can take decisive and speedy actions to address these issues.

> Data, if used well, can have the power to revolutionize how leaders engage their people.

Thanks to recent improvements in understanding human behavior, we can measure an unprecedented amount of information on how to create an environment where everyone is thriving. Using data based on employee feedback, we can scientifically pinpoint areas of opportunity for your business by understanding the drivers of engagement that help people do their best work. While, as a human-centric leader, you will have an established and trusted relationship based on setting goals with your people and understanding their *why*, that is only one piece of fostering true engagement. It's scary to think, but sometimes we have to admit that we don't know what we don't know. No training, podcasts, or even books can prepare you for that. When you combine your intuition with insights from data, you can feel confident you're taking the right actions for your team. And really, why would you make any move without the clarity of data and science when such clarity is available?

While it might seem counterintuitive to what I've written in this book, data is one of your most powerful tools in leading like a human. Data helps you make informed decisions about leading your people and shines a light on the things you may be missing. It can show you in black-and-white detail where the problems are and the best ways to address them. Leading like a human means solving real problems for your people. Data proves that your leadership style is working. You might have followed every tip and trick in this book, but, without data, you don't have a clear picture of your team and the issues they need your help to solve. Data lets you communicate frankly with your people about the problems they face in their day-to-day and how you're going to tackle those problems together. Data is also a strong unifier that rallies your people behind solving a particular problem that affects everyone within your organization. These concrete metrics

> Without data, you don't have a clear picture of your team and the issues they need your help to solve.

give you something real to point to when guiding your managers and can be used to hold them accountable to cultivating engagement at your organization.

Throughout my career, I've seen firsthand the power that data can have when used to solve a business's engagement issues. Based on my experience and the experiences of some of my colleagues, I've compiled in this book a list of best practices that can ensure you're harnessing the full potential of your data. This process will require action from people at every level of your organization so that you can get a holistic view of the issues you're all facing. Before you do anything, however, make sure you identify a trusted partner who can help you make sense of the employee-engagement data along the journey. When collected and used appropriately, data is the most effective tool in your leadership toolbox. If wielded irresponsibly, however, it can do more harm than good.

While this partner will be essential along the way, it's your role as the leader of the organization to create the strategy and to model action from the data. Together, you will **gather employee feedback** that will help you **discover engagement insights**. With these insights, you'll **align your leadership team** to create an action plan that addresses your employees' feedback. Finally, **empower your managers** to execute against this plan, and then **measure again** to see the impact of your work. Taking these five steps will ensure that you are using employee-engagement data to best understand your workforce and how to lead them effectively.

GATHER EMPLOYEE FEEDBACK

As a leader, no one knows your company better than you do, but it's nearly impossible to have the right answer at the right time. The first step to better understanding the situation within your organization is simply to gather your employees' feedback. When you're constructing your survey with your trusted third-party advisor, make sure you know what you're measuring. You need to **ask the right questions to get the right answers**, or else your data might be more confounding than anything else. What are those answers, you might ask? You want to ensure you're getting data that you can act upon. Asking general open-ended questions in your surveys will result in a slew of long paragraph-length responses that will be more overwhelming than illuminating. From asking to move the office closer to their house to new flavors of coffee creamer in the break room to greater 401K contributions, open-ended responses rarely give you the information you need. If you do ask open-ended questions, make them focused on specific areas that the quantitative data has flagged for more context. When creating the survey, make sure your partner is asking questions that will provide you with the most actionable data. Crafting surveys is a difficult thing, and you need an expert who can help ensure you ask the right questions to get information that you can take action on.

While you are ensuring that you're gathering data you can act on, also confirm that you are **measuring the right thing**. Primarily, make sure you are measuring engagement at your organization and not satisfaction. As a reminder, measuring satisfaction is asking those old-school questions: "Are you satisfied with the compensation and benefits?" and "Would you likely recommend working here to a friend?" These kinds of questions will give you data that will be unhelpful in creating an engaged workforce. Another common mistake is asking questions tied to a company award for best culture. Again, these questions tend to ask the wrong questions, and the resulting data is often skewed since employees know an accolade is on the line. Instead, focus on the seventeen psychological drivers I shared in chapter four, or things that focus on the motivation, atmosphere, and focus of your employees.

In order to get the most accurate data, ensure that all surveys conducted are **confidential** so that employees feel comfortable sharing their honest opinions. When you let an outside party run the survey, your employees can feel safe in sharing their honest opinions without fear of repercussion or retaliation. No matter how much your internal team swears they can't (or won't) look at back-end SurveyMonkey or Google Form responses, there will always be a shadow of doubt looming over employees as they respond.

So far, if you've followed the tips above, you know that the information you're trying to measure is accurate because you're asking the right questions and maintaining confidentiality. But looking at hundreds, if not thousands, of data points can be overwhelming, and how do you know exactly where the problem is within your organization? The next-best practice for gathering feedback is to be able to **segment the data by teams**. By sorting your data based on groups within your organization, you'll be able to pinpoint the greatest opportunities for improvement with a clear definition of what that segment of employees will need to increase their level of engagement. Again, not every department may be struggling with rest and need additional time off. Don't implement sweeping actions across the organization because of a few loud voices; instead, slice and dice the data to inform the best action for each segment.

Now we know *what* to measure and, through segmentation, we will know *where* opportu-

> Don't implement sweeping actions across the organization because of a few loud voices; instead, slice and dice the data to inform the best action for each segment.

nities lie in the organization, but another question still looms—*when* should you collect all this information? **Frequency** of measuring data is a tricky question to ask with a very simple answer: make sure you're gathering data in a timeframe that provides you time to analyze the results and take action. Measure too frequently (daily or weekly), and you'll likely feel overwhelmed by the amount of data without enough time to analyze and act while causing survey fatigue among your employees. Measure too infrequently (every twelve or twenty-four months), and you will be behind critical changes in your business. We've found that measuring quarterly is a good rule to go by. This cadence most often aligns to the rapidly changing needs of a business and gives leaders time to communicate and act on the data. We've also found that most organizations set quarterly objectives and KPIs. The quarterly frequency provides leadership with the information they need to create data-driven priorities for the people initiatives.

Understanding the appropriate communication **channel** for sending out your survey will make sure you get the most responses to your survey as possible. It's critical that your survey meet your employees where they are. Let's be honest here: most of your employees are on their phones for a majority of their workday anyway. If your survey isn't mobile friendly, you'll likely see a decrease in participation rate. Plus, many organizations' employees don't have company email addresses. Leveraging mobile and even kiosk functionality allows any employee's voice to be heard regardless of their access to technology. Consider how to reduce as much friction as possible for your employees to access the survey and leverage a multichannel strategy. One caveat, going back to the best practice of confidentiality: do not offer a paper survey option. Oftentimes, paper surveys (especially with any open responses) create skepticism among employees that their responses are not truly confidential. From mailing it in to using a facilitator to tracking handwriting, too many variables are involved that often lead to less honest feedback. Finally, regardless of the channels available, communicate to the team why you value their voice and how important it is for them to respond in order to help inform the improvements for the organization.

DISCOVER ENGAGEMENT INSIGHTS

Using the best practices above can ensure that you have reliable data to analyze so that you can solve the very human problems you're facing. In the responses to your survey, you'll discover engagement insights with your trusted advisor to guide you. At Emplify, we believe humans solve human problems. Behind every data point is a human story that's waiting to be uncovered, which is another reason you should partner with a trusted advisor who can help you make sense of all the graphs, heat maps, and line charts. What hasn't worked is when we see leaders trying to analyze the data by themselves. Not only does this take twice as long, but they often head in the wrong direction, miss the major themes, or worse: do nothing from analysis paralysis. A data expert can review the results at every level of your org chart—from specific teams to divisions to the entire company. From there, you can filter the data even more by key attributes such as generation, location, gender, ethnicity, and tenure to show you what's working, what's not, and where the issues are centralized. Working with another human who knows how to interpret the data and keep you focused on the biggest opportunities means you'll quickly know how to start activating the data.

ALIGN YOUR LEADERSHIP TEAM

At this point in your data process, you'll have a strategic plan based on solid direction from a trusted resource who's helped you sift through your employee-engagement metrics. So now what? A lot of leaders at this point create a never-ending list of people initiatives with the best intentions from what the data has shown, but then three weeks later will pivot or deprioritize these initiatives, only to cross off one or two items. In order to avoid doing this, align your leadership team on one or two of the biggest-impact actions from the results of the data analysis. As Harvard professor and author Michael Porter said, "The essence of strategy is that you must set limits on what you're trying to accomplish." Even with clear insights, execution will fail if senior leaders aren't aligned with a clear scope.

To do this well, you should **tie people metrics to business outcomes** and establish a baseline to demonstrate what success looks like. Executives are data-minded leaders. Directly correlating employee data to business outcomes allows leaders to see how engagement initiatives are affecting other critical metrics. This helps ensure employee engagement is prioritized and that the necessary time and resources are dedicated to moving people projects forward. I hear a lot of leaders think engagement is this fluffy concept that's great to focus on when time allows, but, as soon as there's a big fire or operational need, it immediately gets moved to the bottom of the to-do list. People are at the core of every business function: customer experience, operational efficiency, sales, you name it. When you start prioritizing the right people initiatives, you'll see a lift in the other critical business metrics too. As in everything you measure, be sure to establish a baseline of the key people metrics you're measuring and benchmark the progress you make over time. Data from a single assessment is actionable on its own, but the real magic happens when you measure consistently over time. This process becomes the proverbial finger on the pulse of your organization.

EMPOWER YOUR MANAGERS

Once your executive team is in lockstep, it's time to distribute the data and its insights to the leaders closest to your people. Empower your managers by giving them access to their data and how they, too, should be making data-driven decisions when managing their teams. Show them the connection to the business objectives they own and the baseline information that you've worked on with your leadership team so they can understand the business impacts of engagement. You can't do it alone. Oftentimes, the engagement data requires action from a team lead (versus an executive) to solve the problem. By giving them the tools and the permission to take action on this data, you'll not only make a bigger impact on your organization, but you'll also give your managers the ability to grow. In this way, you encourage the culture of continual improvement you have established based on the tips found in the previous chapter. When you allow the power of data to surge through your organization at every level, you have the power to make huge changes to your organization and its level of engagement.

With all your people leaders aligned, make sure to communicate this process and your decisions to the rest of the organization. It's not just what you do, but how you say something. Executives, be transparent with the results of the survey, regardless of improvement, and share how you're using this data to inform your decisions. Managers, share the data in team meetings and use it as a point of conversation in your one-on-one check-ins. Employees hate surveys because they don't believe their responses will change anything. When you close the feedback loop and make them part of the process, you give even the most apathetic employee hope that things will improve.

THE DATA LIFE CYCLE

Developing clear and focused action plans is great, but it's not enough to hope people do something with them. To truly create a culture of engagement, every leader (including executives) needs to be held accountable for their actions and results. This is why establishing those baseline metrics you created earlier is so important. After collecting, analyzing, and aligning around the data, measure again to see if your actions have helped to address the problem. Continue to leverage your advisor and follow the best practices from above. Not only does this perpetuate your culture of continual improvement, but it also allows you to reprioritize your to-do list and adjust your people strategy to address the biggest threats to the organization. Think about it: Is there any other business function where you review data and results only once a year? If you're anything like me, you have a bookmarked Salesforce dashboard that you refresh at least once a day (maybe even once an hour).

Following this life cycle ensures you're staying ahead of turnover or productivity concerns and taking the right steps for the business. While you might feel you intimately know what's going on within your organization, it's always best to regularly collect data so that you can have clarity on what the issue is and have the confidence to act. Data is a true mirror, and leaders are always surprised when they see the scientific truth of a situation that then eliminates the spin and office politics that can blind even the best of leaders.

CASE STUDY: TH MARINE

To shine a light on what data can really do for your organization, I want to tell you the story of TH Marine and how their data process created an engaged workforce, which resulted in real business impact. TH Marine is a family-owned manufacturing business that produces parts for boats. Unfortunately, their production team—about a dozen employees—were experiencing a massive retention problem. Each year they were experiencing 100 percent turnover of the team, meaning they were consistently recruiting, onboarding, and ramping new folks, only to lose them months later. To figure out why this was happening, they worked with Emplify to conduct a survey of the entire organization. What they discovered was that there were huge utilization problems within this specific team. Bluntly, these highly skilled tradesmen felt their skills were being underutilized and under-valued. This was one of the main reasons the team was disengaged, which then caused their unprecedented turnover rate.

The data had provided insight to TH Marine's leadership about what and where the problem was in the organization, but the leaders didn't necessarily know how to fix the problem. To understand that, they went to the people closest to the problem to find a solution. These employees told leadership that they'd joined to do the work they loved doing—welding and producing the boat parts—but that's not how they were spending most of their time. Instead, they were spending about half their days picking up heavy sheets of metal and moving them from one side of the room to the welding table. This reduced the time they could spend actually producing, and even worse, this manual labor was causing backaches and other physical ailments. Not only did this hamper them from doing their jobs, but it also seeped into their personal lives, to the point where they couldn't even pick up their kids. Their time was being wasted, so they'd leave

TH Marine in search of a new company where they could do good work without straining their bodies. What could leadership do to help alleviate this problem? Buy two products: a hydraulic lift and a leveling table—a onetime investment of about $60,000.

With these two tools and the authority to redesign their work space to better suit their needs, the team was able to focus on what they'd been hired to do. The result? After measuring the workforce again, they found that the production team went from being one of the least engaged teams in the company to the most engaged team. This bump in engagement also created a lift in TH Marine's bottom line. According to their data, they found a 30 percent rise in productivity, equating to $3.8 million dollars per year in additional capacity. This was a win on all sides: the business no longer had a revolving door of employees, and the production team was doing the work they loved. And all that for just sixty grand! Now, not every problem can be solved with a leveling table, but this is a great example of using data to define the problem and then taking specific actions to create better work environments for your people.

Data gives you the ability to act with precision in making business decisions. When you do this, you'll have the clarity and confidence that come from knowing the right action to motivate and encourage your people. In addition, you'll improve the communication you have with your people because you'll know you are talking about the things that they are concerned and worried about. Leaders are always afraid of uncertainty, but data equips them with knowledge so they can act. As the final tool in your leadership toolbox, allow data to serve as the backbone that gives you the confidence to make bold decisions.

ACTIVATE IT!

DEFINE IT

- Seek a trusted third-party advisor to help you gather your data and analyze it quickly.

- Ask questions that measure the right thing and will provide results for easy action.

- Ensure confidentiality so you're getting the most authentic and honest answers from your people.

- Segment data by meaningful subsets of your business to pinpoint specific actions.

LIVE IT OUT

- Measure at a frequency that gives you enough time to act on your data.

- Analyze the data and create an action plan.

- Tie people metrics to business objectives in order to illustrate what success looks like for your leadership and management team.

- Remeasure on a cadence that aligns with how you set business objectives to see the impact of your action plan and where you can reprioritize.

- Communicate to your people the results of your action plan.

MAKE IT YOURS

- What is your business KPI for your people?

- Are you confident that you know the most pressing issues in your organization today?

- What are some unknowns in your business that might keep you up at night?

- Is every people leader in your organization aligned on the right actions to foster employee engagement?

- What are some of the blockers to implementing a measurement process?

- How could you use data to answer questions about your strategy or to reinforce projects or initiatives you've been wanting to implement?

ACTIVATE IT! NOTES

_____

_____

_____

_____

_____

_____

_____

_____

_____

_____

_____

_____

_____

_____

_____

_____

_____

_____

_____

_____

_____

CONCLUSION

Hello, hello! You've made it! You've completed this book and, hopefully, taken away some insights on how to lead like a human. But that's not really the end. I want to congratulate you on taking the reins in your journey toward unlocking your own potential and the potential of the people you lead. For me, that's always been the reason why I do what I do: to help people realize what they could become when they do work that fills their heart, challenges their mind, and engages their hands. I hope you'll continue on this path you've just started and share what you've learned with your colleagues and staff. The process of self-improvement is a continual one and can catch fire when you bring in those around you.

Leadership is a calling. My mother heard it when she was helping her students, I heard it during that first sermon at Commonway, and I'm sure you've had moments like that for yourself. But leadership is also a privilege. You have a commitment to bring out the best in your people, and that's hard work. Trust me: growth takes work, and you're putting in that work right now. But you've got the rest of your life in front of you. Along the way, you'll meet people who are on their own quest toward self-fulfillment. As a human, take a tip out of my mom's book and help them however you can. As a leader, show them how far you've come and how your experience can guide them in becoming their best self. Through this, you'll find yourself changing and becoming more confident, more decisive, and, ultimately, more like yourself. It's a privilege to do this for someone. Never take it lightly.

While this leg of our journey together has come to an end, I hope you continue to reference this book whenever you feel stuck or stalled in your work. If you want to dive even deeper into this work, check out emplify.com/human to download a copy of the facilitation guide that goes along with this book. I've compiled questions, templates, and exercises for you to continue to create an engaged workforce. It's my hope that this guide will help you implement what we've covered here. Remember, leading like a human is a practice— it's something you will continue to grow in and will create many moments for self-examination and reflection. I wrote this book to be a nudge in that direction for leaders like you who are invested in their own journey of growth and where it can take them.

On my own path, I've found inspiration from other media sources that have helped me on my way. One of the first books that comes to mind is *Start with Why: How Great Leaders Inspire Everyone to Take Action*, by Simon Sinek. This book helped me articulate one of the core tenets of my philosophy: creating and actualizing your own personal *why*. Another I'd recommend is *Radical Candor*, by Kim Scott. This book taught me how to be my authentic self as a manager, and how honesty and candor are paramount to creating any stable working relationship. Some other books and media to consider as a next read include *Why Work Sucks and How to Fix It: The Results-Only Revolution*, by Cali Ressler and Jody Thompson; the *Manager Tools Podcast*, by Michael Auzenne and Mark Horstman; and *Scaling Up*, by Verne Harnish. Finally, I cannot recommend enough Jerry

Colona's *Reboot* and the podcast that accompanies it. Jerry and his work have been critical for me in my own self-discovery, and his work helped me take on the role of chief people officer at Emplify. All of these sources have challenged and helped me realize areas of growth in my own leadership.

My journey, by the way, is far from over. I continue to pursue my own personal *why* as the chief people officer at Emplify. Every day, I get to work on challenging problems with people who motivate me to be my best self. I'm still learning, and I'm still growing into the person I was meant to be. If you'd like to follow me on that journey, I (along with some other great leaders at Emplify) will be sharing our cultural experiments, failures, and successes to help others learn what can help their organizations in our Emplify People Lab. Connect with me on LinkedIn to follow along in the journey. There might be a time when a new challenge will call to me, but for now, I couldn't be happier than where I am. When that time comes, I know I'll be equipped to take on that challenge with my heart, my head, and my hands. And I want to charge you to do the same. If you need it, I'm giving you the permission to do so. You're taking the first step in a journey that lasts a lifetime. Be your very best self, see the best in your team, and lead them in unlocking their own potential. In doing so, you will not only create a loyal, high-performance team, but you will also be the type of leader you can be proud of. You'll experience difficulties along the way, but don't let them deter you. Find the *why* that drives you, and become the leader you were always meant to be.

And remember to lead like a human.

ADAM WEBER works every day to help people realize and achieve their full potential. As the chief people officer and cofounder of Emplify, he helps lead an innovative, highly engaged culture and shares his learnings with strategic people leaders all over the world. Throughout his life, Adam has taken on various roles in the pursuit of helping people become their best. These include the pastor of a small church, an entrepreneur of a digital startup, and even a traveling musician.

In addition to his position at Emplify, he is an expert and speaker on employee engagement, culture, team performance, and leadership development. In an effort to share his experience with others, he has spoken at a number of events around the country for which he has been consistently rated as a top presenter. In 2020, Adam was named to Business Insider's list of Rising Stars in Human Resources.

Adam is a proud Ball State University alum, holding a bachelor's degree in sociology and a master's degree in organizational communication. He lives with his wife, two sons, and dog in their net-zero house in Zionsville, Indiana. His hobbies include camping with his family and backyard birdwatching.

OUR SERVICES

At Emplify, we're on a mission to help all people achieve their true potential at work. We provide simple assessments for employees, clear guidance for executives, and actionable coaching for managers.

There has long been a fundamental misalignment between employees' feedback and leaders' ability to act on it. For sixty years, employees have been taking surveys and waiting for their leaders to do something. And for sixty years, leaders haven't had the right tools or guidance to act quickly and with confidence.

That's where Emplify comes in. Combining the simplicity of technology with the experience of consulting, Emplify works with you to find out what's really going on with your people and create the change your business needs to move forward. Emplify's method weaves together software and services to support all people leaders at every step of their journey.

STEP 1: GATHER EMPLOYEE FEEDBACK

Employees need a simple and confidential way to share the truth about their work experience with the leaders who can make a difference. Surveying employees can be a logistical nightmare, so we take that burden off your shoulders.

STEP 2: DISCOVER PEOPLE INSIGHTS

A good survey will confirm a few hunches and uncover some blind spots, but expert data analysis will reveal the story beneath the surface. Trust your People Insights Consultant to decipher the data and take you down the right path.

STEP 3: ALIGN YOUR EXECUTIVE TEAM

Even with clear insights, execution will fail if senior leaders aren't aligned. Your People Insights Consultant will present a third-party perspective on wins and risks to your entire executive team so they walk away unified with clear action priorities.

STEP 4: EQUIP MANAGERS TO ACT

From executives to frontline managers, we ensure people leaders have the coaching and resources they need to take action within their own teams. You can't do their job for them, but you can make it easier.

To learn more, go to **emplify.com/human**.

Printed in the USA
CPSIA information can be obtained
at www.ICGtesting.com
JSHW012034140824
68134JS00033B/3055